CULLODEN
1746

Major Gillies McBean (see p. 83).

CULLODEN 1746

BATTLEFIELD GUIDE

Third Edition

STUART REID

Pen & Sword
MILITARY

An imprint of
Pen & Sword Books Ltd
Yorkshire – Philadelphia

First published in Great Britain in 2005 by
PEN & SWORD MILITARY
An imprint of
Pen & Sword Books Ltd
Yorkshire – Philadelphia

Second edition 2011
Third edition 2018

ISBN 978 1 52673 973 5

Typeset in 9pt Palatino by Mac Style

Printed and bound by CPI Group (UK) Ltd, Croydon, CR0 4YY

Pen & Sword Books Ltd incorporates the imprints of Pen & Sword Archaeology, Atlas,
Aviation, Battleground, Discovery, Family History, History, Maritime, Military, Naval,
Politics, Social History, Transport, True Crime, Claymore Press, Frontline Books,
Praetorian Press, Seaforth Publishing and White Owl

For a complete list of Pen & Sword titles please contact

PEN & SWORD BOOKS LTD
47 Church Street, Barnsley, South Yorkshire, S70 2AS, England
E-mail: enquiries@pen-and-sword.co.uk
Website: www.pen-and-sword.co.uk

Or

PEN & SWORD BOOKS
1950 Lawrence Rd, Havertown, PA 19083, USA
E-mail: Uspen-and-sword@casematepublishers.com
Website: www.penandswordbooks.com

Contents

Maps

Map key

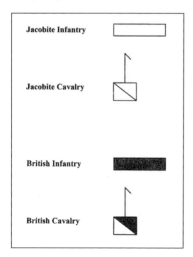

CHAPTER I

Prince Charles and the '45

The '45: the Jacobite Rising of 1745 is unquestionably the best known and most evocative episode in Scottish history, but rather than retell the old story with all its whys and wherefores, causes and consequences, this book aims simply to provide a straightforward account of the battle of Culloden, based on the very latest research and archaeology. That story is still pretty much as told in the first edition of this work, published in 2005, but since then the battlefield itself has been revealed anew thanks to an extensive programme of works by the National Trust for Scotland and the final chapter has therefore required fully updating.

Nevertheless, every story has its beginning and some of the whys and wherefores had a direct influence on how, why and where the battle was fought, so it is as well to start by briefly looking at how the whole business came about.

The Stuarts, their supporters and their songwriters were prone to laying stress on their claim to be the rightful, lawful kings of Britain; but in England at least that claim was a sick joke. They came to the English throne almost by default with King James VI, and left it with his grandson exactly eighty-five years later in 1688. What was more, over twenty of those years had been taken up with a particularly vicious and destructive cycle of civil wars which left deep scars on the English political psyche, and it was a reopening of those scars which sent the last King James hurrying into exile. It was at best a shaky claim to legitimacy, and a second restoration fifty years on was never going to be a realistic goal. Yet one of the tragedies of the '45 is that that was exactly what Prince Charles Edward Stuart aimed at, to the undoubted detriment of his chances of re-establishing the dynasty in Scotland.

Even in Scotland it may have been too late, for the Stuarts had all but abandoned the country in 1603. King James VII was not driven from his throne by an unjust, casual usurper, but by the judgement of a Scottish parliament standing up to a dictatorial – and absentee – monarch. As long ago as the famous Declaration of Arbroath in 1329 it had been very firmly established that the King of Scots ruled only by the will of his people, and that ultimate constitutional authority lay with

Prince Charles Edward Stuart as imagined by the Victorian artist Robert McIan. As always, McIan's depiction of clothing styles is accurate, but sadly there is no evidence that the Prince wore a kilt until he was a hunted fugitive after the campaign was over.

parliament as the representative of the people, and not with the man (or woman) who happened to wear the crown. The great civil war of the 1640s began with the Scots' repudiation of royal authority, and by the end of the century the Stuarts were just as unpopular with large sections of the Scottish population as they were in England. Furthermore, while the English parliament uneasily represented King James's flight to France as a de facto abdication, its Scottish counterpart rather more robustly declared that he had 'forfaultit' the Crown and offered it instead to his Protestant son-in-law, William of Orange.

Neither William nor those who succeeded him were forcibly imposed upon Scotland, and it has long been accepted by historians that Culloden was not a straightforward battle fought between a Scottish army and an English one. By the end of the campaign there were easily as many, if not more, Scots fighting for King George as were fighting for the Stuarts, and yet there is no doubt that in a way it was such a battle. Sir Walter Scott best captured the truth in his novel *Waverley*, written when memories of those far-off unhappy times were still very much alive. As Scott told it, those who donned the white cockade and marched behind the Bonnie Prince's white banner were consciously fighting for Scotland. It was, however, for the old Scotland, the repeal of the Union of 1707 and a king at Holyrood rather than St James that they fought for, rather than the new outward-looking Scotland trembling on the brink of the Enlightenment and the Industrial Revolution. The rising began in the Highlands, not because the clans – or at least some of them – were the staunchest and most faithful supporters of the old Ayrshire family which produced the Stuart dynasty, but rather because they were among its last remaining ones. The starkest and most symbolic irony of the '45 is the fact that the Jacobites' first and most famous victory was won not on a heather-covered hillside, but on a flat Lothian cornfield at Prestonpans, and that the tartan-clad swordsmen who surged forward in the way of their ancestors to defeat the red-coated Lowland Scots of General Cope's army had first to run across a railway track.

In Scottish terms, then, it came down in the end to a battle between the past and the future, and as such the result was probably inevitable. All that sustained the Stuarts' fading claim to the throne was a lingering resentment at the Union between the two kingdoms of Scotland and England in 1707. At the time it had been bitterly unpopular, based on the one hand on Scotland's bankruptcy after the Darien venture, and on the other on a need for Scottish soldiers in a continental war which threatened a similar disaster for England. This was something the Jacobites were quick to seize upon, for while the Stuarts had in the end proved both remote and widely unpopular they had at least been kings of an

The prospect of a Stuart restoration was far from appealing to many Scots, such as these Edinburgh volunteers sketched by an artist from Penicuik.

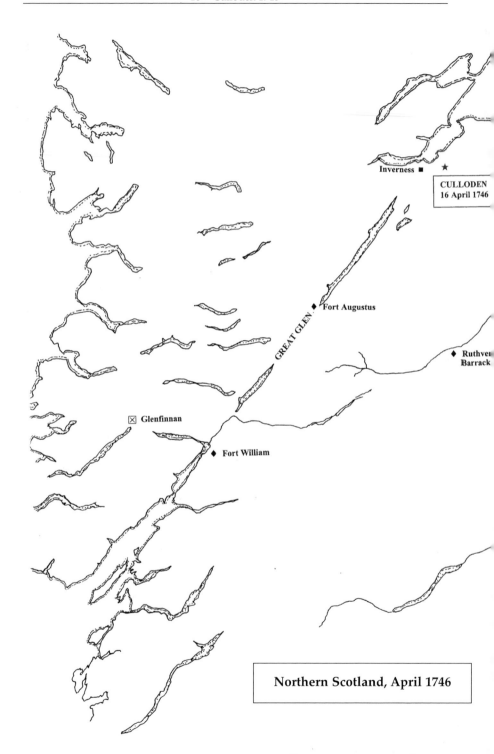

Inverness ■

★

CULLODEN
16 April 1746

GREAT GLEN

♦ Fort Augustus

♦ Ruthven
Barrack

⊠ Glenfinnan

♦ Fort William

Northern Scotland, April 1746

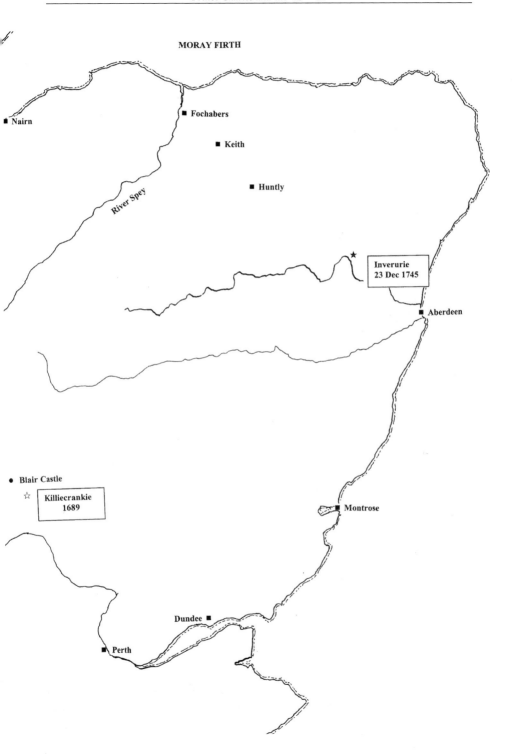

MORAY FIRTH

Nairn

Fochabers

Keith

Huntly

River Spey

★ Inverurie
23 Dec 1745

Aberdeen

Blair Castle

☆ Killiecrankie
1689

Montrose

Dundee

Perth

independent Scotland, and they tried to capitalize on this in launching both the promising but unsuccessful risings of 1708 and 1715. Nevertheless, although considerable, albeit sentimental, opposition to the Union continued in the years afterwards at a grassroots level, its commercial and political benefits were becoming increasingly apparent to those with the energy, capital and vision to exploit them. Assessments by Jacobite agents in the late 1730s starkly concluded that if another attempt to recover the throne was not launched soon, support for the Stuarts would be lost by default. Even more worryingly, most of those few who were prepared to commit themselves to the cause bluntly stated that outside assistance was essential, and that they would only rise in the event of a French landing.

The fact of the matter was that times really were changing. A hundred years before, during the great Civil War, the countryside on both sides of the Highland Line was awash with arms and with men who knew how to use them, for or against the King. Now it was very different. The last battle between rival clans was at Mulroy back in 1688 – two generations before Prince Charles, the Young Pretender, arrived. Highland gentlemen might occasionally strut around with broadswords on their hips in defiance of the Disarming Acts, and some of the rougher, more criminally inclined elements might still try to 'lift' cattle from time to time, but there was no longer any real experience of battle – by 1745 even the dreadfully mismanaged debacle of Sheriffmuir lay thirty years in the past. Moreover, those who had seen something of warfare, whether in the ranks of the British Army or even a foreign one, were only too well aware of the level of drill and training now required on the modern battlefield. The Highland chiefs might still reckon on being able to pull their men out onto the heather, and by and large their faith would not be misplaced when the time came. None of them, though, were under any illusions about whether those tenants, sub-tenants and 'followers' could really be called soldiers, which was why they wanted the French.

Unfortunately, the French displayed very little interest in crossing the sea to Scotland or anywhere else, for their long land frontiers encouraged French generals and French armies to look eastwards to the Rhineland and the plains of Lombardy, or north to the age-old battlegrounds of Flanders, rather than embark on uncertain amphibious ventures. Nevertheless, when British troops intervened in Germany at the behest of the Elector of Hanover – who had the great good fortune to be King George II of England and Scotland as well – a substantial invasion force was put together in readiness in 1744 for a descent in the Thames estuary, while a smaller force was to sail for Scotland. However, this was only ever conceived as a diversionary operation rather than a serious attempt to assist the Stuarts, and when the inevitable Channel storms disrupted the embarkation and scattered the fleet, the attempt was abruptly abandoned. The troops gratefully marched north into Flanders instead, leaving behind them Prince Charles Edward Stuart, the elder son of the would-be King James.

Born in Bologna in 1720, the 'Young Italian', as his enemies delighted in calling him, was handsome, charismatic and unquestionably the best and brightest hope of his fading house. Brought up to expect that one day he would have to fight for his father's throne, he took an obvious interest in soldiering, but his education was

One of McIan's surprisingly accurate, albeit romanticized, depictions of a Highland gentleman.

The Prince in a rather more conventional eighteenth-century pose. The armour might be anachronistic, but the 'Young Italian's' clothing is rather more convincing than McIan's Highland dress.

The man who would be king: Charles Edward led the uprising on behalf of his father, the would-be King James III and VIII.

a haphazard affair which left him ill-prepared for its practical aspects. In short, as the campaign would demonstrate all too clearly, his enthusiasm for military operations was not matched by a corresponding level of technical expertise, and his otherwise commendable determination ultimately blinded him to the practical difficulties of achieving his objectives. Unfortunately, this in turn led to a certain degree of instability and was manifested in a tendency to abdicate all responsibility for the management of his army in times of crisis. Had he gone ashore as a guest of the French army in the suite of the famed Maréchal de Saxe, as was intended, this might not have mattered, but now he was on his own and with no obvious means of getting across the Channel, let alone to Scotland.

Then, in the summer of 1745, the Prince was offered help from what at first sight seems an unlikely source. When the Stuarts fled abroad at the end of the seventeenth century they did not go alone, and there was by now a substantial colony of Irish exiles in Brittany, largely clustered around the ports of Nantes and St Malo. Many of the exiles were ship-owners, and Lord Clare, the commander of the French army's famous Irish Brigade, introduced some of them to the Prince. A consortium headed by Walter Routledge and Anthony Walsh had once been engaged in the slave trade between Africa and the West Indies. This, however, had been seriously disrupted by the war and so they had turned to privateering or licensed piracy instead. While British privateers found, outfitted and manned their own ships, French ones, curiously enough, could hire real naval vessels, which meant that the Irish consortium had access to ships which were big enough to carry soldiers and military equipment to Scotland. And so, for an unspecified price they set sail from Belle Isle on 5 July 1745.

There were two ships in the beginning, a large but elderly naval frigate named the *Elisabeth* and a smaller commerce raider, *Le du Teillay*. The first carried a company of infantry and most of the arms and ammunition, while the second carried the Prince and his staff. Unfortunately, the shoestring expedition was intercepted by HMS *Lion* while rounding the tip of Cornwall, and a long battle ended with both the *Lion* and the *Elisabeth* shattered and limping for home. Thus the Prince sailed on alone and landed on the Hebridean island of Eriskay on 23 July to an unexpectedly unfriendly welcome. Far from bringing the French army which the chiefs demanded, he had just seven companions and hardly any cash or equipment. Not surprisingly the local chiefs, such as MacDonald of Sleat, flatly refused to join him, and instead the Prince was rather brusquely advised to turn around and go home again. Retorting that he *had* come home, he moved on to the mainland and there entered into a desperate round of negotiations with some of his other potential supporters. All of them took a very great deal of persuading before Cameron of Lochiel finally tipped the balance. The rebel standard was not raised until nearly a month later, at Glenfinnan, on 19 August. By that time, the government was only too well aware of what was going on, and Lieutenant General Sir John Cope, Commander-in-Chief Scotland, had been ordered into the Highlands to deal with the matter before it got out of hand.

With the war in Flanders then at its height, the forces actually available to Cope were far from impressive either in numbers or in quality. Even on paper he could

Regimental Designations

Until the middle of the eighteenth century the British Army's regiments were usually known by the name of their colonel, or rather colonel-in-chief, but while some did lead their regiments at Culloden in person, this was becoming increasingly rare. Although the numbers allotted to each regiment did not assume a primacy until after 1751, they have been used in this book in order to avoid confusion, particularly where a regimental colonel changed in mid-campaign. The 37th Foot, for example, was officially designated Monro's Regiment, until its colonel (a Highlander, as it happens) was killed at Falkirk. Afterwards it passed to Louis Dejean and is sometimes referred to as such, while other accounts of Culloden continue to refer to it as Monro's.

Occasionally the numbers themselves can be confusing. Ordinarily at the end of a war the size of the army would be reassessed and any regiments surplus to requirements disbanded strictly in reverse order of seniority. In 1748, however, a colonial regiment and ten regiments of marines were 'reduced' out of sequence, with the result that all the surviving units junior to the 41st Foot were renumbered. Those which served during the Culloden campaign are therefore represented by double numbers. The Black Watch, for example, appear as the 43rd/42nd Foot, the first being the number which they actually bore in 1746 and the second the more familiar number which they inherited in 1748.

muster little more than three and a half battalions of infantry and two regiments of cavalry. However, one of those battalions, Guise's 6th Foot, was completely scattered, garrisoning the various Highland forts while two companies of another regiment, Lascelles's 58th/47th Foot, were in Edinburgh Castle. For obvious reasons it was also considered impractical to take the two dragoon regiments into the hills, and so in the end Cope assembled only one complete battalion: the ten companies of Murray's 57th/46th Foot, together with eight companies of Lascelles's 58th/47th, five companies of Lee's 55th/44th Foot and two Additional (or depot) companies of recruits for the 43rd/42nd Highlanders. It is worth mentioning, incidentally, that almost all of his men were Scots. The Highlanders, the famous Black Watch, were obviously Scottish, but even the three line regiments – Lee's, Murray's and Lascelles's – had actually been recruited in Scotland. Only Guise's Regiment, up in the Highland forts, was unambiguously English, having recently been brought up to strength in Warwickshire and elsewhere in the Midlands.

Marching from Stirling on 20 August, Cope hoped to augment this little force with substantial numbers of loyalist volunteers, but all he actually succeeded in picking up en route was an incomplete company of recruits for a new regiment, Loudoun's 64th Highlanders. Nevertheless, notwithstanding this apparent apathy, Cope did at least have access to a very efficient intelligence network, and at Dalwhinnie he received definite information that the rebels planned to fight him in the steep traverses of the Corrieyairack Pass. Rightly judging this position to be far too strong, Cope abandoned his original intention of establishing a forward base at Fort Augustus, at the top of Loch Ness, and instead marched north to Inverness.

At the time Cope really had very little choice, although he was careful to secure the backing of a council of war for the decision. The fact of the matter was that the rebels were blocking the road to Fort Augustus, yet remaining where he was, in the hope that the rebels would come out and fight, was hardly a realistic option, especially as supplies were already running low. In purely military terms it would probably have made some sense to fall back and adopt a better blocking position further south, but in political terms such a retreat would have been absolutely disastrous. Inverness was a far from satisfactory compromise, yet in the end it made no real difference. Disappointed in their sanguine expectation that the General would obligingly march into the trap prepared for him, the rebels were initially thrown off balance by this move. Their immediate reaction was to follow the General to Inverness, but eventually the temptation of simply marching directly on Edinburgh proved too much for them. Masking the move with an unsuccessful assault on Ruthven Barracks outside Kingussie on 29 August – it was held against them by just twelve men under a Sergeant Terry Molloy – they moved south and took, or rather walked into, Perth on 3 September. After resting up there for a week they set off again, crossed the Forth on 13 September, and then in very mysterious circumstances managed to seize Edinburgh on the night of 17 September 1745.

Ironically, having reached Inverness, Cope meanwhile was at last joined by some useful reinforcements. He had already taken a company of Guise's 6th Foot from Ruthven Barracks, and now he found another in Inverness, together with three more incomplete companies of the 64th Highlanders and, most promising of all, a 200-strong loyalist battalion raised by Captain George Monro of Culcairn. Only too aware of the danger to the capital he was supposed to be protecting, Cope then marched hard for Aberdeen, hurriedly embarked all but Culcairn's battalion on ships there and arrived off Dunbar on 17 September. He was quite literally just 24 hours too late to save Edinburgh, but, still determined to retrieve the situation, he got his men ashore and marched westwards until, finding the rebels considerably coming out to meet him, he halted on a flat cornfield outside Prestonpans on 20 September.

From Cope's point of view he had found himself an ideal position with clear fields of fire for his infantry and artillery, and no impediments to hinder a charge by the two regiments of dragoons which had rejoined him at Dunbar. In theory he had everything going for him, but ironically it was a blunder on the part of the inexperienced rebel commanders which was to quite inadvertently cost him the battle.

For their part the Jacobites had taken up what appeared to be their own ideal position on Falside Hill, immediately to the south, from where they thought they could charge down on Cope's army in the approved manner. Unfortunately, when taking a closer look, however, the rebel commanders discovered to their dismay that a bog, known as the Tranent Meadows, lay at the foot of the hill and would effectively stop any charge in its tracks. After some shuffling around, and a lot of noisy recrimination, the rebels eventually decided to swing around to their right under cover of darkness and attack Cope from the east. The move got off to an inauspicious start when barking dogs alerted the General to the fact that something was happening, and when the rebels crossed the bog by a supposedly little-known track they found it covered by a picquet of dragoons. As luck would have it, the dragoons' commander, Colonel James Gardiner, was not only a local man but actually owned the land in question and was therefore well aware of the existence of the path.

As a result, Cope and his men were soon alerted to what was afoot, and, far from being caught asleep as the popular song suggests, were ready and waiting for the rebels, deployed behind a colliery railway track or wagon-way crossing an 'extensive corn field, plain and level, without a bush or tree'. It was still to all intents and purposes a textbook position, and, with his right flank securely anchored on the Tranent Meadows, and the coal pits and houses of Cockenzie discouraging any large-scale movement around his left flank to the north, Cope ought to have felt secure.

On his left flank was Hamilton's 14th Dragoons, then forming his centre; Murray's 57th/46th Foot; Lascelles's 58th/47th (now including the two companies of Guise's 6th); and the half-battalion of Lee's 55th/44th. On his right flank were six little curricle guns and four small Coehorn mortars, together with an artillery guard drawn from the infantry battalions, and finally Gardiner's 13th Dragoons. His Highland companies, tasked with guarding the baggage, were securely ensconced in Cockenzie kirkyard some distance to the north. All in all, and including those Highlanders, Cope had 1,464 infantrymen and 567 cavalrymen, exclusive of officers.

They did not have long to wait. A loyalist volunteer from Edinburgh, named John Home, recalled that: 'Harvest was just got in, and the ground was covered with a thick stubble, which rustled under the feet of the [Jacobite] Highlanders as they ran on, speaking and muttering in a manner that expressed and heightened their fierceness and rage. When they set out the mist was very thick; but before they had got half-way, the sun rose, dispelled the mist, and showed the armies to each other.'

What it also showed was that the rebels had blundered in their deployment. They divided themselves in two wings: the right, comprising three battalions of MacDonalds under the Duke of Perth, and the left, comprising the Camerons, Stewarts of Appin and Perth's Regiment under Lord George Murray, with a small reserve made up of the two battalions of the Atholl Brigade – a Perthshire formation normally accounted as a Lowland unit. Together the front-line units totalled some 1,750 men, while the reserve under Lord Nairne added another 500. Cope's infantry were therefore heavily outnumbered, although conversely the rebels had nothing to oppose his cavalry but a mere 36 troopers hanging about in the rear, well out of harm's way. Nevertheless, it was the cavalry who were attacked first, for in the hurry to deploy in the mist the two front-line divisions became widely separated, so when they went forward they each attacked the outer flanks of Cope's army. Thoroughly intimidated by the sheer weight of numbers thrown against them, the dragoons and artillerymen fled, leaving the infantry with no enemy to their front and their flanks wide open. The Highlanders then simply rolled up the infantry line and, as Major John Severn of Lascelles's afterwards testified, 'A large Body of their Left rush'd on obliquely on our Right Flank, and broke the Foot as it were by Platoons, with so rapid a Motion, that the whole Line was broken in a few Minutes.'

In those few minutes the British Army lost some 150 dead and 1,326 prisoners, while the rebels on the other hand admitted to 5 officers and 30 men killed, and another 70–80 wounded. It was by any accounting a famous victory, but it is worth emphasizing the point that the rebels deliberately chose to fight and win on a field far flatter than the one which would later be criticized at Culloden, and against an army which boasted a far larger proportion of cavalry and artillery than the Duke of Cumberland would enjoy.

After Prestonpans the Jacobites returned to Edinburgh to savour their triumph and recruit their forces, but despite their bombastic claim to be masters of Scotland, their actual position was far from secure. On the credit side they had beaten Cope, occupied the capital and set up their own administration in much of eastern Scotland. On the other hand, with the exception of the tiny barracks at Inversnaid – little more than a glorified police station – they had not captured a single garrison

A tough-looking character identified by the Penicuik artist as 'Skiteraluck the Younger' – possibly McGhie of Shirloch, a captain in the Atholl Brigade.

or post, and that uncomfortable fact was periodically underlined by the guns of Edinburgh Castle. Ideally the Jacobites' first priority should have been the consolidation of their embryonic regime in order to establish and afterwards defend an independent Scotland, but at Newcastle upon Tyne, Field Marshal George Wade was overseeing a much larger concentration of veteran troops recalled from Flanders. Therefore it was resolved to march south and deal with the British Army before the loyalists could assume a significant domestic threat.

The march to Derby, and the successful return to Scotland, was undoubtedly a considerable achievement in itself, but when the rebel army marched out of Edinburgh on 31 October 1745 it still had no clear objective. At Dalkeith two options were debated. The Prince favoured the direct approach of marching into Northumberland and bringing Wade to battle as soon as possible. In retrospect this would almost certainly have been the better option, but instead it was decided to avoid an immediate confrontation and instead push south into Lancashire in the twin hopes of triggering an English uprising and winning time for French intervention. Although Prince Charles had convinced himself by the time the rebels reached Derby that London was within his grasp, the other Jacobite leaders took a more realistic view, as Lord Elcho recalled in his account of the fateful council of war there:

Lord George told him (the Prince) that it was the opinion of Every body present that the Scots had now done all that could be Expected of them. That they had marched into the heart of England ready to join with any party that would declare for him, that none had, and that the Counties through which the Army had pass'd had Seemed much more Enemies than friends to his Cause, that there was no French Landed in England, and that if there was any party in England for him, it was very odd that they had never so much as Either sent him money or intelligence or the least advice what to do ... Suppose even the Army march'd on and beat the Duke of Cumberland yett in the Battle they must lose some men, and they had after the King's own army consisting of near 7000 men near London to deal with ... that certainly 4500 Scots had never thought of putting a King upon the English Throne by themselves.

Thus they turned back, fought a brisk little rearguard action at Clifton near Penrith on 18 December and, having left a garrison in Carlisle, recrossed the border into Scotland two days later. Ostensibly the garrison's purpose was to hold open a

Hogarth's famous depiction of the march to Finchley is a typically tumultuous scene which provides a completely misleading impression of what was actually quite a formidable army assembling to defend London.

gateway for a renewed incursion into England, but this can have been no more than a cynical encouragement to the doomed defenders. Their real task was to delay Cumberland, which they succeeded in doing until 30 December.

Once back in Scotland the rebels faced an interesting tactical situation. They had no sooner abandoned Edinburgh exactly two months before than it was reoccupied by a brigade marched up from Berwick by Brigadier General Handasyde. Briefly appointed Commander-in-Chief North Britain, Handasyde was an energetic officer who quickly added a regularly enlisted provincial battalion raised in Edinburgh, two more loyalist volunteer battalions raised in Glasgow and Paisley, and a fourth from Stirling. With this force he was able to hold the Forth Crossings and so prevent a second Jacobite army under Lord John Drummond from marching south until the Prince and his men returned to occupy Glasgow. At that point the loyalist brigade commanded by the Earl of Home retired with the regulars on Edinburgh, while the Jacobites decided to seize the strategically important town of Stirling to serve as their own base for the coming winter.

Unfortunately, the Jacobites were defied for a time by the burgh's militia, and although the loyalists agreed to surrender after a brief stage, Stirling Castle did not, and within the week General Hawley was on the march with three regiments of dragoons, numbering about 800 troopers; 12 battalions of regular infantry, totalling 5,488 officers and men; and another 1,500 loyalists and a rather scratch train of artillery. Having heard that he was on his way, the Jacobites scaled down their siege of the castle and prepared to meet him on nearby Plean Moor. Hawley, however, moved forward very cautiously and encamped at Falkirk, where he was joined on 17 January by the Argyle Militia. This slow approach created a very real problem for the rebels. It was now the middle of January and the weather conditions made it quite impossible to keep the army concentrated in the open. Yet if they dispersed into their quarters they obviously ran a very considerable risk that Hawley would lunge forward and destroy them in detail. In short, the only real alternative was to take the offensive themselves.

Three battalions under the Duke of Perth and old John Gordon of Glenbuchat were left behind to maintain the blockade of Stirling, but most of the army, comprising the Highland Division under Lord George Murray, and a number of Lowland units intended to form a second line were committed to the operation. Lord John Drummond, with the cavalry and a little battalion of French regulars made up of detachments or 'picquets' drawn from his own Royal Ecossois and three Irish units, was at first sent off by a different route as a diversion, but once he had rejoined the main body the total strength of the rebel army came to something in the region of 5,800 infantrymen and 360 cavalrymen.

Hawley had underestimated his opponents and was taken completely by surprise, but, warned just in time by a loyalist scout named Sprewel, he got his army moving and galloped up onto the nearby Burgh Muir of Falkirk, a steep hill which overlooked his men's position. There he discovered the Jacobites coming on fast, and a desperate race began to secure the summit. Hawley's three cavalry regiments, all commanded by Colonel Francis Ligonier, reached the top first, but the infantry, formed in two lines each of six battalions, were still breathlessly lagging behind as they bent into the stiff climb up broken ground. In order to gain time, therefore, Hawley ordered Ligonier to charge the rebel right wing immediately without waiting for support.

As some of the rebels later admitted, the unexpected appearance of the dragoons caused dismay as they came over the crest, and the Jacobite front rank immediately fired a hasty volley at long range, seemingly without doing any damage. However, another volley delivered by the second rank at point-blank range was much more effective, and a loyalist volunteer named Corse recorded seeing 'daylight' appear in the dragoons' ranks. Many of Cobham's 10th and Ligonier's 13th Dragoons immediately swerved aside, although a number of Cobham's pressed on and burst straight through one of the MacDonald battalions to rout Lord Ogilvy's men, who were standing in the second line. Unfortunately, Hamilton's 14th Dragoons simply turned around and bolted straight back down their side of the hill. In the process they rode over Corse and the rest of the loyalist Glasgow Volunteers, while they in their turn quite understandably responded by shooting up the fleeing dragoons.

To make matters worse, all four MacDonald battalions then scattered in pursuit of the dragoons and at the same time the rest of the rebel front line surged forward after them. In a moment of high drama, just as they came flooding over the crest, a wild storm broke, blowing hard in the faces of Hawley's infantry, who were still toiling up the hill. In the circumstances it is hardly surprising that some of them panicked and ran without firing a shot.

To all appearances the Jacobites were on the point of winning another dramatic victory like Prestonpans, but, having been largely hidden from each other until this moment, the two armies were considerably misaligned, and while the MacDonalds and Lochiel's Camerons outflanked Hawley's left, the British right wing similarly outflanked the Jacobite left. Tellingly it was only the outflanked regiments of the left wing – Edward Wolfe's 8th, Blakeney's 27th and Monro's 37th – that actually broke, and so suffered the heaviest casualties. Some of the regiments in the centre conformed by falling back in their turn, perhaps rather more hastily than they should have done, but they remained in good order, came off more or less unscathed and soon recovered their composure at the bottom of the hill. Ironically their retreat contributed to the disaster which now overtook the Highlanders. As ever the retreating troops exercised a fatal attraction and instead of fighting those who remained, nearly all the Jacobites streamed down the hill in pursuit. Then, amid all the confusion Brigadier General James Cholmondley ordered Barrell's 4th and Ligonier's 59th/48th to swing backwards and pour a succession of volleys into the rebels' now exposed flank.

This brought about an immediate and dramatic change of fortunes as the rebels stumbled to a confused halt and then ran away in their turn. As their Irish Adjutant General, Colonel Sullivan, disgustedly recalled: 'the cursed hollow square came up, took our left in flanc & obliged them to retire in disorder. There was no remedy nor succor to be given them. The second ligne, yt HRHs counted upon, went off, past the river & some of them even went to Bannockburn, & Sterling, where they gave out yt we lost the day.' To all intents and purposes they had, for not only did half of the front line and most of the second line run away, but Brigadier Cholmondley was soon joined by some of the dragoons and by Major General Huske, who also brought up three more infantry battalions. Thus reinforced the Brigadier proposed a full-scale counter-attack, but he was overruled by Huske, who wanted to wait for Brigadier Mordaunt to bring up the rest of the army from the bottom of the hill. In the meantime Lord George Murray, the senior Jacobite officer on the field, was having no success at all in recalling the MacDonalds, although Colonel Sullivan eventually managed to bring up the little battalion of French regulars, who by this time were probably the Jacobites' only remaining formed body of troops. As it grew darker and wetter, and with no real sign of the opposing army, Huske declined to engage them and retired back to the camp, more for want of anyone to fight than through any sense of having been beaten.

For a time Hawley considered holding on to the camp, for by now he and Brigadier Mordaunt had managed to rally most of his broken regiments. It was in fact an old Roman campsite, still surrounded by the remains of earthworks, and could have been defended easily enough, but in the darkness and driving rain no one had much enthusiasm for the idea, and so he fell back first to Linlithgow and then to Edinburgh. This gave both the Jacobites and friendly historians sufficient excuse to claim a victory, but in reality it had been a very close rerun of the Battle of Sheriffmuir in 1715, where, as the old song famously said, 'We ran and they ran, and everybody ran away man.' Neither side had actually suffered many casualties. The Jacobites admitted to some fifty killed and sixty to eighty wounded, while the British Army apparently lost about seventy killed, although that included twenty officers. That unusually high proportion, as they admitted, was simply down to the officers' having been deserted by their men, and most of the casualties belonged to

Doune Castle, north of Stirling, was used as a prison by the Jacobites after Falkirk.

The tower of St Ninian's Kirk, Bannockburn. Used as a magazine by the Jacobites, the church was blown up when they retreated northwards after Falkirk, and the tower is all that remains.

the three regiments – Wolfe's 8th, Blakeney's 27th and Monro's 37th Foot – that were outflanked and broken by the Camerons and Stewarts.

Large numbers of officers and men on both sides had in fact simply scattered far and wide across the countryside, and for much of the night the Prince and many of his officers were convinced the battle had been lost. Consequently, although they soon moved into Falkirk itself, the rebels were quite incapable of pursuing the retreating redcoats and displayed no real elation at their pretended victory. By contrast, although the British Army was under no illusions that it might actually have won the battle, neither its officers nor its men considered themselves to have been beaten. Instead, once they had dried out and been resupplied, they marched westwards again under the newly arrived Duke of Cumberland. This time the rebels declined to fight and instead raised the siege of Stirling Castle and hastily retired northwards.

CHAPTER II

The Battle That Never Was

From this point onwards the Jacobites' aim should have been to avoid any major operations until the spring brought in fresh recruits, and hope that in the meantime a combination of dark nights and dirty weather would help French blockade runners to bring reinforcements, arms, ammunition and money. In the short term, however, having been turned out of Stirling, they had to secure an alternative base, and since Perth was too vulnerable, the next obvious choice was Inverness. Accordingly, at Perth the army split in two and while both the Lowland Division and the cavalry, commanded by Lord John Drummond, retired up the east coast, through Aberdeen, the Highland Division led by Lord George Murray marched directly on Inverness.

Cumberland, too, temporarily went into winter quarters of his own. Leaving a recently arrived Hessian contingent and most of the Argyle Militia at Perth to cover the Highland roads, and so prevent a repeat of the previous year's dash on Edinburgh, he followed the Lowland Division up the coast as far as Aberdeen. Then, while it continued its retreat in the teeth of a howling blizzard he halted there and put his army into cantonments for some four weeks.

An officer and sergeant (identified by sash and halberd respectively) of one of the British Army's Highland regiments.

Although the British Army had now gone into winter quarters, which was a polite way of saying all major operations were shut down until the weather improved and the troops were properly resupplied, it was not the end of the fighting. Indeed, if anything it actually now spread and intensified, albeit at a lower level.

For the Jacobites, their first priority was still to find themselves a proper base, and with the Lowlands abandoned that really meant capturing Inverness. Ironically, however, the Highland capital, far from being the hotbed of rebellion which popular legend might suggest, was instead currently serving as the home for a sizeable loyalist army. Largely made up of the Highland Independent Companies and some less formally organized clan levies, such as Monro of Culcairn's battalion, it was commanded by Colonel John Campbell, Earl of Loudoun. By its very existence this loyalist army exposed the fallacy that the Highlands were solidly behind the Jacobites, and indeed it is significant that after the first contingents marched south with the Prince to Prestonpans and Derby, comparatively few clansmen were recruited to his cause thereafter. In part this was of course because most of the genuine volunteers had 'come out' at the very beginning of the rising, but afterwards, with Inverness in loyalist hands and soldiers of the Independent Companies fanning out from the Great Glen forts, it became physically difficult actually to recruit fresh men for the Prince. On the contrary, the Independent Companies themselves proved both an attractive alternative and a refuge from those Jacobite recruiting parties who increasingly preferred intimidation to persuasion. Nevertheless, Loudoun's military operations were far from impressive, for while he was a good administrator who

In marked contrast: a distinctly unheroic looking clansman after the Penicuik artist.

had served as Cope's adjutant general, he was quite out of his depth when in independent command. Some ten years later, while serving as Commander-in-Chief North America, he would be rather unkindly compared to the figure of St George on tavern signs: always on horseback but going absolutely nowhere.

So it was in Scotland during the rising. Having recruited and equipped what could have been an effective army, Loudoun plainly had no idea what to do with it, other than to sit tight at Inverness. The only serious operation which he mounted was an attempt to recapture Aberdeen from the Jacobites just before Christmas 1745. At the very last moment, however, he himself decided to lead an irrelevant (and quite ineffective) punitive sweep into the Frasers' country, while leaving the far more important Aberdeen operation to be commanded by the inexperienced Laird of Macleod. He for his part got as far as Inverurie, just 10 miles short of Aberdeen, with about 500 men, and then halted to wait for reinforcements. Eventually Monro of Culcairn turned up with another 200 levies and, though leading the smaller contingent, assumed command of the whole expedition by virtue of his regular commission. Another 500 men were still expected under the

Provost Skene's house in Aberdeen. This was the Duke of Cumberland's headquarters while his army was cantoned in the area.

Laird of Grant and, unwilling to provoke a fight in the meantime, Culcairn refused to send out scouting parties. Although he was almost certainly correct in fearing that once out of his sight they would start plundering and so raise the countryside against him, the inevitable result was that the rebel army turned up like the devil at prayers – just when they were least expected.

Having grimly scraped together every single man they could lay their hands on, including a little contingent of French regulars, the Jacobites proceeded to attack and utterly

Robert Gordon's College, Aberdeen. This newly built school was palisaded around and turned into a fort when Cumberland marched north.

rout Culcairn's Highlanders at bayonet point just after sundown on the night of 23 December.

Despite their own poor operational security, the absence of any scouts meant that the rebels quite literally caught Culcairn and his men napping. Those of the loyalists actually quartered in the village itself were only just able to get themselves formed up before the battle began, but those scattered around the outlying farms never came up in time. With 900 men the Jacobites decided to attack the village from two sides at once, but as it lay at the confluence of the River Don and the smaller River Urie, that entailed crossing by two quite different fords in the dark. They were therefore taking a considerable risk, but in the event the loyalists took up a central position between the two and at too great a distance from both to contest the crossing. Thus attacked from two directions the loyalists quickly fled, and very few were killed or wounded on either side. Most men in both armies appear to have either taken cover or run away at the first exchange of fire, and the only real check to the Jacobite attack came when in the moonlight they mistook an earth bank for a row of men and 'fired very successfully into it'. Unsurprisingly, the debacle provided a salutary shock to the loyalists, especially as the victorious rebels were Lowlanders. In the end both sides were happy to attribute the outcome to the fact that the loyalists had no broadswords – 'their darling weapon' – an ingenious excuse which satisfactorily explained Macleod's defeat, on the one hand, and yet preserved the myth of Highland invincibility, on the other.

Thereafter things quietened down again, but now, on learning that the Jacobites were approaching Inverness, Loudoun for once took decisive action and on 16 February set off under cover of darkness to attack the rebel headquarters a little to the south of the town at Moy Hall. Once again, however, the operation ended in an even more discreditable shambles than before, which was ever afterwards celebrated as the 'Rout of Moy'.

Legend has it Loudoun's advance guard was ambushed by a blacksmith and three other men, and that the whole lot of them very promptly ran away. In reality there was rather more to the affair, but if anything it was even more discreditable to all concerned – on both sides. Loudoun's own account was remarkably honest in describing what happened, first to the detachment and then to his main body:

> we marched to the heights above the water of Nairn, when to my infinite mortification, saw and heard about a mile on my left, a running fire from the whole detachment. They saw, or imagined they saw, four men, on which they made this fire. But the consequence on the main body was very bad, for it threw us into the greatest confusion. I got my own regiment, at the head of which I was in the front, saved from falling out of the road. All faced to where they saw the fire. They were ten men deep, all pressed, and a good many dropping shots, one of which killed a piper at my foot, whilst I was forming them. The rest fell back out of this road in a considerable way. It was utmost confusion, and it was a great while before I could get them brought up and formed; and the panic was still so great that it was with the greatest difficulty when the party came in, in twos and threes, that I could, standing before the muzzles of their pieces, prevent their firing on them.

Worse still, once he began counting noses, it soon became apparent that five of the companies at the rear of his own column had completely disappeared. It can have been small comfort when it later transpired that only one company had actually run away, while the others, led by an extremely short-sighted officer, had simply followed rather hopefully after them. In the meantime, having hung about for an hour or so, Loudoun eventually came to the remarkably obvious conclusion that although there was no further sign of the Jacobites, the operation had clearly been compromised, and so he retraced his steps to Inverness.

Nevertheless, the rebels had nothing very much to boast of either. In the first place they were taken completely by surprise, having being warned of Loudoun's approach at quite literally the last moment. It also speaks volumes that as 1,500 heavily armed soldiers closed in, all that could be found to stop them were four men who were not even in the rebel army. Nor, despite later stories loyally emphasizing the Prince's sang-froid, were things much better up at the Hall. There he and his staff – and his hostess, Lady Mackintosh – were rushing around in a panic, and the only result of the affair was that the Young Pretender, having bolted into the February darkness in his nightshirt, came down with something akin to pneumonia. This, however, can have been scant consolation to Loudoun, for with the coming of daylight the rebels got on his track and hustled him straight out of Inverness and across the Beauly Firth to the Black Isle.

Having at last secured for themselves the proper base which they so badly needed, the rebels then set about consolidating their position with a variety of minor operations. Naturally enough these were aimed at finishing off Loudoun and reducing the various Highland forts, while covered by the Lowland Division, cantoned at the little village of Fochabers, on the River Spey.

The Highland war began promisingly enough for the rebels. Ruthven Barracks and its little garrison, now commanded by *Lieutenant* Molloy, had already surrendered on terms on 11 February after old John Gordon of Glenbuchat brought up some artillery. So anxious were the Jacobites to erase their earlier defeat that they even allowed Molloy and his men to remain in unmolested occupation until the Prince himself turned up, whereupon they gave their paroles and marched off to Perth. Alone among the officers who surrendered their posts during the rising, Molloy escaped a court martial. It was a very different story at Inverness, where Major George Grant of the Black Watch surrendered the castle with far less excuse on 20 February, while Fort Augustus followed suit on 5 March, after a French mortar shell scored a direct hit on the fort's magazine, and completely demolished one of the bastions in the process. After that, however, it all started to turn sour for the rebels. The third of the big 'chain' forts in the Great Glen, Fort William, determinedly held out against a mixed force of Highlanders and French regulars, and elsewhere the various other rebel detachments found themselves bogged down in lengthy operations which really ought to have been completed within a few days.

A major priority for the Jacobites was of course to deal with the Earl of Loudoun's forces, who had by this time retired further north to Tain in Ross-shire. Unfortunately, since the Earl had very sensibly taken all the available boats over

A figure from Major George Grant's New Highland Military Discipline *of 1757, a drill book written in an unsuccessful attempt to rehabilitate the Major, who was dismissed from the service for surrendering Inverness Castle to the Jacobites in 1746.*

The plan and internal elevation of Ruthven Barracks as it was in 1745/46.

to his side of the water, the rebels were obliged to march the long way around the head of the Cromarty Firth. This delay gave Loudoun ample time then to ferry his army across the water to Dornoch. This meant the rebels then had to turn back and march around the head of the Dornoch Firth, whereupon Loudoun frustrated them again by shipping his men directly back over the firth to Tain. Loudoun was no military genius and his rag-tag soldiers were hardly elite troops, but for all that they were doing pretty well at keeping the rebels occupied. This frustrating dodging about continued for some time until Lord George Murray gave up in disgust, but in the end on 20 March the Duke of Perth and Colonel Sullivan gathered enough boats of their own along the Morayshire coast for a surprise amphibious assault. Despite the first wave getting lost in thick fog, turning around and mounting a very resolute assault on the beach they had just embarked from, the operation eventually turned out to be a complete success. Loudoun's forces were not only caught unawares but the same fog prevented them concentrating to mount a counter-attack on the beachhead. Instead they fled without fighting, but although some led by Loudoun himself retreated westwards and eventually took refuge on the Isle of Skye, others retired northwards with quite unforeseen results.

With their work apparently done, Perth's men were recalled to Inverness, but then on 24 March fate quite unexpectedly intervened in the shape of a French blockade runner named *Le Prince Charles* which was forced ashore by the Royal Navy at Tongue, in the very far north of Scotland. On board were a

The Duke of Perth, as depicted by McIan after a contemporary portrait.

number of officers, a picquet of the Irish Régiment de Berwick and no less than £12,000 in badly needed gold. This was loyalist country and far from Inverness, but nevertheless the French gallantly decided to try to get through. Unfortunately the smell of the gold aroused the intense interest of everyone for miles around. Some of Loudoun's men, a company of the 64th Highlanders, who had retreated up that way, got to it first, and although they afterwards put it about that the French had most unfortunately succeeded in dumping it all in a nearby loch before surrendering, no one was in any doubt it was actually jingling in the loyalists' pockets. A Jacobite brigade commanded by the Earl of Cromartie was therefore sent north in what turned out to be a vain attempt to recover it. In the end they gave up and turned back, but by that time it was too late: not only were they absent when the climactic battle of the campaign was fought at Culloden, but they themselves managed to get ambushed and dispersed by other loyalist troops in almost farcical circumstances the day before.

Meanwhile, further south Lord George Murray had embarked on a series of minor operations of his own, afterwards remembered as the Atholl Raid. The Hessian troops based at Perth were themselves covered by a screen of small outposts, manned for the most part by the Argyle Militia, and in the early hours of the morning of 10 March Murray's men briskly captured all of them except Blair Castle. This was held by a company of the regular 21st Scots Fusiliers, commanded by the redoubtable Sir Andrew Agnew. At this point it would probably have been sensible for Murray to have called it a day and quit while he was ahead, but Blair belonged to his brother, the Duke of Atholl, and he himself had been brought up there, so injured pride as much as military necessity led him to embark on a full-blown siege of the castle. Unfortunately, his artillery proved to be useless – one of his two guns stubbornly refusing to shoot straight – and this operation, together with fending off the increasingly aggressive Hessians, not only detained Murray there for three fruitless weeks but completely dislocated the plan to concentrate the army on the Spey in good time to meet Cumberland's advance.

The Duke, meanwhile, first established a ring of outposts beyond his own cantonments in and around Aberdeen, and soon pushed a complete infantry brigade and some cavalry, commanded by Major General Humphrey Bland, out as far as the burgh of Huntly, in order to mark Lord John Drummond's nearby base at Fochabers. Inevitably there was a certain amount of bickering between the two sides, culminating on the night of 20 March with a heavy Jacobite raid on the village of Keith, halfway between the two. The raid was well planned under the direction of a French officer, Major Nicholas Glasgoe, and turned out to be a complete success. The village was occupied by a mixed party of about seventy men of the Argyle Militia and just over thirty of Kingston's 10th Horse, all commanded by a Captain Alexander Campbell of the 64th Highlanders. It would actually appear they had no business being there at all and should instead have been mounting a standing patrol in the debatable lands. Instead, however, Campbell had seemingly hatched a plan to mount a raid on Fochabers, but, as so often happens, the rebels got their retaliation in first. Glasgoe assembled a mixed party comprising fifty men of John Roy Stuart's Regiment, a similar contingent of Lord Ogilvy's

Regiment, sixteen 'French' regulars from the Régiment de Berwick, and twenty hussars. Swinging right around the village undetected and approaching it from the east, Glasgoe and his men were at first mistaken for friendly reinforcements. The result was a sharp little fight to capture the kirkyard where the main guard was posted, but most of the Highlanders and the cavalrymen were asleep and taken without resistance. As usual there were few actually killed on either side, although Captain Campbell was wounded and then quite viciously beaten up after first escaping and then being recaptured. All in all fifty-three of the Argyles and thirty-one of Kingston's Horse were returned as killed or missing, only five of the latter escaping.

Otherwise nothing of any real consequence occurred for the next three weeks. The Jacobites were therefore caught off guard when Cumberland suddenly lunged forward with his whole army during the second week in April. Immediately after the affair at Keith on 20 March Cumberland had reinforced his forward base at Huntly and sent the Earl of Albemarle to take command. Designated the 1st Division, Albemarle's force eventually comprised Cobham's 10th Dragoons and Kingston's 10th Horse, and the 1st and 3rd Infantry Brigades, a total of two regiments of cavalry and six battalions of infantry, besides the obligatory scouts from the Argyle Militia. Their orders were to remain at Huntly until 10 April to cover the movement of the rest of the army into its jumping-off positions.

This volunteer was sketched in the Penicuik area, but could equally well represent one of the Jacobites serving in Lowland regiments such as Lord Ogilvy's.

A recreated company of British regulars. An infantry battalion would consist of ten of these.

Meanwhile, Brigadier John Mordaunt with the three battalions of the 5th Infantry Brigade and four cannon (all temporarily designated as the 2nd Division) moved up to Old Meldrum, north-west of Aberdeen, on 23 March, but the operation proper did not begin until the morning of 8 April. On that day Mordaunt's 2nd Division marched due north to Turriff, while Cumberland with the 3rd Division (Ker's 11th Dragoons and the 2nd Infantry Brigade) took their place at Old Meldrum, and Lord Sempill, commanding the independent 4th Infantry Brigade, moved to nearby Inverurie. Although the weather was improving, this widely dispersed march seems to have been aimed at ensuring sufficient covered accommodation could be found for the troops and their horses, but it may also have ensured that a largely hostile countryside was suitably overawed, as well as confusing the rebels as to their intended line of march.

The company of regulars from Campbell's Royal Scots Fusiliers left behind to garrison Aberdeen were supplemented by a local militia who, like these Edinburgh volunteers, lacked cartridge boxes and other accoutrements, but were at least issued with captured Spanish muskets.

If so the effort was largely wasted, for the very speed of their advance meant that they escaped detection. The rebels were certainly aware of an increase in activity but attributed it to vigorous patrolling, and never penetrated the heavy screen of Highlanders and cavalrymen to detect the heavy columns moving up behind. Next day both Cumberland and Mordaunt moved on to unite at the coastal town of Banff. Then, with still no sign of movement on the part of the rebels, the whole army concentrated further along the coast at Cullen on 11 April. Fochabers was just a short distance away, and not unnaturally Cumberland and his officers anticipated that the crossing of the Spey there would be fiercely contested.

In fact, thanks to the abysmal failure of their scouting, the Jacobites were taken completely by surprise. News that Cumberland had left Aberdeen certainly led to orders being given for the Highland Division's concentration at Inverness, but even so the speed of the British Army's advance caught them off balance. Murray took some time to call in his men scattered all over Atholl; some of the western clans were still besieging Fort William, others were chasing the French gold up in the north, and far too many had simply gone home. Only the Lowland Division remained in place but far from alert. Some of their cavalry claimed to have detected Cumberland's forces on the night of 11 April, but somehow the message was never passed back up the line. Consequently, the Duke of Perth, his brother Lord John Drummond and some of their officers were at breakfast at the manse in Speymouth on the morning of 12 April when:

a country man came over the River in great haste and told them that the Enzie [a local name for that area] was all in a 'vermine of Red Quites'. But they were so averse to believe it, that when they ran to an eminence and observed them at a great distance they swore it was only muck heaps: the man said it might be so, but he never saw Muck heaps moving before.

An undignified scramble then ensued as Fochabers was evacuated and the rebels withdrew to a hutted encampment, known as 'the barracks', on the west side of the river. Unfortunately, strong as it was, the position was still unfortified and worse still, as Cumberland approached, it was occupied by only some 2,000 men, comprising the cavalry, the Lowland regiments and a little over half the French regulars. They even were completely without artillery support, but nevertheless with a little more resolution they might still have been able to contest the river crossing. The Spey is famously the fastest running river in Scotland and the ford, as one trooper recalled, was a very bad one:

> having loose Stones at the Bottom, which made it very difficult for Man or Horse to step without falling; the Water Belly-deep, and very rapid; the Ford not lying right across, we were obliged to go Midway into the River, then turn to the Right and go down it for about sixty yards, then turn to the Left, inclining upwards to the Landing Place.

There were in fact three different fords used by the British Army that day: one below Garmouth, another at Gordon Castle and the third at the kirk of Bellie. Yet the only opposition they faced was a scattering of pistol shots fired by the last of the rebel cavalry, who just crossed ahead of them, and the only loss was one dragoon and four women swept away and drowned. Cumberland himself wrote from Speymouth next day that 'It is a very lucky thing we had to do with such an enemy, for it would be a most difficult undertaking to pass this river before an enemy who should know how to take advantage of the situation.' Instead, covered by a rearguard of Lord Lewis Gordon's men – identified by their white colours – the rebels burned their hutted camp and rapidly fell back first towards Elgin and then to Nairn. After weeks of relative inactivity, events were suddenly moving very fast. Having heard that Cumberland was on the move, Colonel Sullivan rode out to assess the situation for himself on 14 April and was disagreeably surprised to find Drummond, and his brother the Duke of Perth, actually in the process of evacuating Nairn as well. Uncomfortably aware that the Highland Division had still not yet reached its concentration area at Culloden, Sullivan therefore ordered them to halt and take up a covering position while he himself took the cavalry out on a reconnaissance.

The Colonel did not need to go far before he realized the true seriousness of the situation, for the redcoats were coming on fast, but in order to give the Drummond brothers more time to get across the bridge at the far end of the town he formed up his little force – a troop of Lifeguards under Lord Balmerino; a squadron of red-coated French regulars, Fitzjames's Cavalerie, under Captain Robert O'Shea; and the hussars under Major John Bagot – all in a single line in order to make as brave a show as possible. Once across the bridge the rebel infantry formed up again and Sullivan, uneasily aware of how badly outnumbered he was, naturally assumed that they in turn would cover his own withdrawal across it. To his chagrin, however, as soon as he fell back to the bridge nearly all the infantry simply turned around and marched off leaving him in the lurch. Fortunately, a small picquet from the Régiment de Berwick waited for him, and, as soon as the cavalry were safely across, a cartload of peat was jammed across the middle of the bridge and set on fire by the unnamed sergeant in charge of the picquet. However, peat is slow burning stuff and it proved to be an ineffectual obstacle, but 'Sullivan continued his retraite making volte face from time to time alternatively with the small number of horse he had & those five and twenty men of Berwicks.' Repeated calls for more infantry support went completely unheeded, but after a couple of hours the British cavalry gave over their pursuit and fell back on Nairn, where Cumberland was establishing his headquarters.

Tomorrow was the Duke's birthday and so he declared a day of rest before beginning the final advance on Inverness, where the rebel army must either make its last stand or disperse into the hills. While he himself took quarters in Nairn's high street, Cumberland encamped his infantry on a flat area of ground at Balblair, just to the west of the town. His cavalry, however, were cantoned out at the little village of Auldearn, two miles away to the south-east. This had been the scene of a bitterly fought battle in April 1645 which eventually ended in victory for the Marquess of Montrose and the House of Stuart. If Cumberland or any of his officers were aware of this association they made no mention of it. Instead the present move, however, was aimed simply at providing the three regiments of cavalry with access to sufficient forage and grazing. Nevertheless, had things turned out only a little differently that night, the tactical significance of their position would have been enormous.

Cumberland's decision to stand fast at Nairn at first seems rather surprising since he must have known or at the very least suspected that the rebel concentration was still incomplete and that a vigorous continuation of the offensive on 15 April might still catch them unprepared. On the other hand, judging by later events, he probably feared that if he did push straight into their concentration area they might instead disperse rather than stand and fight, perhaps committing him to a long summer campaign in the hills. What he needed was a decisive blow to end the rebellion then and there in order that he could take his army back to Flanders before the French came out of winter quarters to renew their offensive against the Dutch barrier fortresses.

The Jacobites had in fact seriously considered falling back. Lochiel's Camerons had come in only the day before, and a delay of even a couple of days, Lord George Murray argued, would see the army swelled by as many as 2,000 men, even without Cromartie's Brigade, which as it happens was at that very moment being ambushed and effectively destroyed at Dunrobin. Cluny and his MacPhersons, however, were still on the march, as were Keppoch's men, the Frasers, and some reinforcements for Glengarry's Regiment, which had just been combed out of Glen

A Highland clansman demonstrating the use of the plaid as an overcoat as well as a nether garment.

Urquhart. Yet in the end if Cumberland chose to continue his advance there was no real alternative but to fight. Although romantics and armchair strategists (or 'cabinet practitioners', as they were called in the eighteenth century) are prone to holding that they should have retired into the hills instead and there conducted a guerrilla campaign, the Jacobites themselves were under no illusions about their ability to sustain one. Murray afterwards grumbled that they had only fought at Culloden to protect their baggage, but in reality the rebels had little choice. Lacking the gold lost in the north, they had no money with which to buy food and therefore had to hang on at all costs to the magazine of oatmeal and salt beef painstakingly gathered in Inverness. Without that oatmeal they would starve, and indeed the clearest answer to those advocating a partisan war is the fact that when Lochiel and the other surviving rebel leaders reassembled their forces for that very purpose after Culloden, they were immediately forced to disperse them again since it was impossible to feed them.

There was no alternative but to fight.

CHAPTER III

Night March

A ccordingly, early on the morning of 15 April the rebels drew up in order of
battle on an open stretch of moorland on a ridge above Culloden House, in
a position which effectively covered both roads into Inverness from the
east. They certainly occupied the highest ground in front of the town, but as a
potential battlefield it was not to everyone's liking. Unsurprisingly, the earliest
critic was Lord George Murray, who unequivocally declared that 'I did not like the
ground: there could never be more improper ground for Highlanders.' His
trenchant opinion has cheerfully been seized upon and endlessly repeated by
subsequent historians – without much thought being given as to how qualified he
was to deliver it. While there is no doubting Murray's personal bravery and powers
of leadership, his actual abilities as a soldier never matched his own conceit of
them, and his criticism of the Culloden site flies in the face of the fact that those
selfsame Highlanders, led by him, had won their most famous victory on an even
flatter and more exposed field at Prestonpans.

Furthermore, Murray's own choice of battlefield was a good deal worse. On
learning that Cumberland had crossed the Spey he hastily picked what he regarded
as an ideal position close by Dalcross Castle, but Colonel Sullivan, while he was
riding out to Nairn on 14 April, turned aside to reconnoitre 'this famiouse field of
Battle', and his professional soldier's opinion of it is worth quoting at some length.
'It was the worst that could be chosen for the highlanders & the most
advantagiouse for the enemy,' he began, unconsciously echoing Murray:

> There is a Ravin or hollow that is very deep & large that goes in zig zag,
> formed by a stream that runs there … I ask yu now that knows the highlanders
> whither a field of Battle, where there is such an impediment as that Ravin was,
> wch is impractical for man or horse, was proper for highlanders whose way of
> fighting is to go directly sword in hand on the enemy? Any man that ever
> served with the highlanders, knows that they fire but one shot & abandon their
> firelocks after. If there be any obstruction that hinders them of going on the
> enemy all is lost; they don't like to be exposed to the enemy's fire, nor can they

A figure which appears to have been intended by McIan to represent Lord George Murray.

resist it, not being trained to charge [load] as fast as regular troops, especially the English wch are the troops in the world that fires best. If I was to chuse a field of Battle for the English, or if they were to chouse it themselves they could not chuse a better, for there are no troops in the world but what they overcome in fireing, if yu don't go in sword in hand, or the bayonett among them.

It is difficult to argue with that assessment, particularly since Murray's only real experience of battle before 1745 had been the ignominious debacle at Glenshiel in 1719. There a Highland army had attempted to fight defensively just as Murray was proposing to do at Dalcross, and had been thoroughly thrashed for its trouble. Sullivan's principal point, that in order for a Highland charge to succeed the clansmen actually needed a clear open field on which to run at the enemy, is unanswerable. Should the British Army come looking for a fight it would do so on ground well adapted to Highland tactics, while if Cumberland marched straight for Inverness he would find the Jacobites on his flank.

Lord George Murray
Born in 1694, Lord George Murray had the unusual distinction of having two brothers simultaneously holding the title of Duke of Atholl. One, Duke William, sometimes also known by his other title as Earl of Tullibardine, was a Jacobite, while the other, Duke John, supported King George. Murray's own background reflected this duality and excited suspicion from the very outset. In 1715 he threw up a regular commission as an ensign in the Royal Scots to join the Jacobites, although he contrived to be absent when the Battle of Sheriffmuir was fought. He did, however, return to fight at Glenshiel in 1719, but was pardoned in 1726, and in 1745 actually tried without success to raise loyalist volunteers for Sir John Cope's army. His defection to the rebels came rather late in the day and, although he was appointed one of the army's rather extravagant allowance of three lieutenant generals (the others being his brother Duke William and James Drummond, Duke of Perth), many Jacobites regarded him with considerable suspicion, and for long afterwards there was a popular tradition in the Highlands that he was a traitor. One of his officers, James Johnstone, perceptively summed him up as 'vigilant, active and diligent; his plans were always judiciously formed, and he carried them promptly and vigorously into execution. However, with an infinity of good qualities, he was not without his defects: proud, haughty, blunt and imperious, he wished to have the exclusive disposal of everything and, feeling his superiority, would listen to no advice.' His rival the highly professional Colonel Sullivan regarded him as an over-enthusiastic amateur, an opinion amply borne out by his ill-conceived night attack on the British Army's cantonments around Nairn on the night of 15 April. At Culloden, however, he fought bravely as a brigade commander, and afterwards escaped into exile in Holland, where he died in 1760.

First, however, there was to be one last tragic blunder. By noon on 15 April Jacobite cavalry patrols confirmed that the British Army was still at Nairn and showed no signs of moving that day. The Jacobite concentration was still incomplete at this time, and some officers resurrected the notion of taking the opportunity offered by Cumberland's inactivity to break contact, abandon Inverness and retire into the hills, or at least take up another position on the other side of the River Nairn. Although the latter option might uncover Inverness, it was argued that Cumberland would not move on the town while the Jacobite Army was positioned on his flank. However, Lord George Murray suddenly changed tack completely and advocated mounting a surprise attack on Cumberland's camp that night.

Murray himself was afterwards extremely disingenuous about the whole affair. His own memoirs simply but quite dishonestly remark that: 'It was then proposed a night attack might be attempted. His Royal Highness and most of the others were for venturing it, amongst whom I was.' This has been sufficient for some historians to throw all the blame for the debacle that followed onto the Prince and the usual scapegoat, Colonel Sullivan. In fact, Lord Elcho quite explicitly recorded how, far from agreeing to the notion simply because anything was better than fighting in the open, it was Murray himself who forcefully advocated the plan in a hectoring speech which:

> enlarged upon the advantages Highlanders have by Surprising their Enemy, and rather Attacking in the night time than in day Light, for as regular troops depended intirely upon their discipline, and on the Contrary the Highlanders having none, the Night was the time to putt them most upon an Equality, and he Concluded that his Opinion was that they Should march at dusk of ye Evening, So as the Duke should not be aprised of it, that he Should march about the town of Nairn and attack them in their rear, with the right wing of the first line, while the Duke of Perth with ye left Should attack them in front, and the Prince Should support the Duke of Perths attack with the Second line.

Unfortunately, it is unclear whether the rebel scouts had discovered that Cumberland's cavalry was cantoned out at Auldearn. There are indications, however, that they might have done, and it is therefore all the more surprising that no one seems to have considered that, though 2 miles away from the town, it was thus perfectly placed to intercept Murray's division as it swung around to the south of Nairn – or worse still to come in on his rear after he was committed to the assault.

In the event it never even got that far. Having proposed the plan, Murray had effective control over the operation and proceeded to demonstrate just how much of an amateur he really was. It was of course intended to be a surprise attack, but remarkably little preparation was made to ensure its success. There was, rightly, some concern that any movement from the Culloden position would be detected by the various naval vessels and transports coming in to anchor in the firth below. Similarly there was more than a shrewd suspicion that loyalist patrols might be operating in the area to the west of Nairn. On the face of it this precluded any major movement in daylight, although no consideration appears to have been given to

A Highland officer as depicted by Robert McIan.

slipping quietly off the crest of the moor and into the valley of the Nairn, which would have very effectively screened the rebels from naval telescopes at least. Worse still, nothing was done to prepare the troops themselves. None of them had been fed since early the day before, and, though they remained on the moor throughout the daylight hours of 15 April, no attempt was made to bring forward any of the precious meal stored at Inverness. One of the Lifeguards, an English volunteer named John Daniel, recalled that 'a biscuit' was given to each of them for 'refreshment', and they may have been the lucky ones.

When Murray first proposed waiting until dusk before starting, some doubts were raised by his colleagues as to whether the army would then be able to cover the 8 miles to Nairn before daybreak. With a confidence which wholly belied his lack of experience in such matters he immediately responded that he would 'Answere for it', but as soon as the regiments did begin assembling for the move, it was found that:

> a vast number of men had gone off on all hands to get and make ready provisions; and it was not possible to stop them. Then, indeed, almost everybody gave it up as a thing not to be ventured. His Royal Highness was extremely bent upon it, and said that, whenever we began the march, the men would all be hearty, and that those that had gone off would return and follow.

The reality was very different and 'when the officers who were sent on horseback to bring them back came up with them, they could by no persuasion be induced to return again, giving for answer they were starving; and said to their officers they might shoot them if they pleased, but they could not go back till they got meat.' Needless to say, the callous indifference by the Prince to the state of his men and his misplaced confidence that all would be well if they simply muddled through simply amounted to wishful thinking. James Johnstone, who in his time had been an aide-de-camp to Murray, then a company commander in the Duke of Perth's Regiment and now a volunteer in Glengarry's, thought that the army was ordered to set off at about eight o'clock in the evening, but Lord Elcho reckoned it was nearer nine. The only benefit from the delay was that it gave time for Keppoch and his men to rejoin the army, although since they had presumably been force-marched to reach Culloden their feelings on immediately being ordered to take part in the operation can easily be imagined.

Still concerned to preserve operational security, Murray ordered the heather set on fire to create the impression they were still encamped on the moor, and then set off across country in order to lessen the chance of tripping any outposts or picquets. In ordinary circumstances this would obviously have been much more sensible than marching straight down the road towards Nairn. The problem was that time was already running out. His optimism was in part founded on the fact that the Highlanders 'had often marched more than two miles an hour', hence his calculation that 'they could have reached Nairn before two o'clock'. Unfortunately, that calculation was at best based on the similar manoeuvre which preceded the victory at Prestonpans, when the army had been moving along Lothian roads rather than across trackless moorland. Moreover, contrary to Murray's cheerful assertion that the Highlanders' lack of 'discipline' would stand them in better stead in the darkness than regular troops, the reverse was actually true. All night operations, and particularly those involving the movement of large bodies of troops, invariably require very thorough planning and preparation if they are to be successful, and, above all, demand a very high standard of 'discipline' or training from those soldiers actually involved. None of these conditions were fulfilled as the rebel army lurched into its last disastrous offensive.

On setting off, the army, headed by an advance party of thirty local men from Lady Mackintosh's Regiment, was organized in four divisions, or rather brigades, one following behind the other. The first, naturally enough, was led by Lord George Murray, the second by Lord John Drummond and the third by the Duke of Perth. Although their composition is nowhere explicitly stated, they were presumably made up of the units which those officers would command the next day, making up the right wing, centre and left wing respectively of the rebel front line. The fourth division, led by the Prince himself, was the reserve comprising the cavalry, the Lowland regiments (with the exception of the Atholl Brigade, which was now attached to Murray's division) and the French regulars.

From the very outset not only was progress slow, but large gaps soon began to open up between the four divisions and eventually between the individual units as a succession of obstacles was crossed. Murray had no hesitation in throwing the blame for these delays on the 'heavily-laden' French troops supposedly toiling in the rear. In reality they were no more or less heavily equipped than anyone else that night. He then went on to complain that: 'The moor they went through was more plashy than expected, and they were obliged to make some turns to shun houses, and there were two or three defiles that took a great deal of time to pass.' That was the real problem of course, instantly familiar to anyone who has conducted a night march. Those numerous obstacles or 'defiles' such as drystone walls invariably took far longer to get across than in daylight, and then once across a regiment would hurry on to catch up, heedless of those still trying to follow after. The fact that it was not only dark but foggy as well only made matters worse, and, though Sullivan says there were officers 'posted all along the road that the Colomn past by, to make every body follow, that they may not mistake their way in the moor,' the gaps grew progressively worse.

Murray, still confidently expecting to get his men outside Nairn by two in the morning, complained bitterly as message after message came up the line requesting him to slow down or halt while the rest of the army closed up. However, as his one-time ADC James Johnstone recalled:

> This march across country in a dark night which did not allow us to follow any track, had the inevitable fate of all night marches. It was extremely fatiguing and accompanied with confusion and disorder. The Highlanders, who could not keep together from the difficulty of the roads, were more or less dispersed and we had many stragglers. As there were a great many bad places to cross, it would have been impossible for the best disciplined troops to have preserved anything like order.

So much for Murray's fatuous notion that the Highlanders' lack of discipline would be an asset, and since Johnstone would later go on to serve with the French Army in Canada, he at least knew what he was talking about when he came to write his memoirs.

The plan had called for Murray's division to cross the Water of Nairn 2 miles below Culraick, then swing around to attack Cumberland's camp from the southeast, while Perth and Drummond simultaneously mounted a straightforward frontal assault. However, by the time Murray reached Culraick, dawn was little more than an hour away. 'The guides though they knew the ground very well,' he complained, adding one more set of scapegoats, 'yet were not judges what time it would take.' With the army still held up crossing the park walls around Culraick Wood, one of his ADCs, Colonel Ker of Graden, was sent back down the line to remind everyone to make the attack sword in hand 'as it would not alarm the enemy so soon'. When he returned to the front of the column, however, he found Murray and his officers 'halted a little to the eastward of Kilravock House, deliberating whether or not they should proceed ... or return to Culloden, as they had not at most, or thereabout one hour to daylight; and if they could not be there before that time, the surprise would be rendered impracticable'. Some were still surprisingly aggressive, and some bright spark daringly suggested that it 'was better to make the attempt with four thousand men before daybreak, than with double the number after it was light'. However, since Murray at that moment could find only some 1,200 men belonging to the Atholl Brigade and Lochiel's Camerons, this was not particularly helpful. What was more, in view of the time they had taken to cover the 6 miles to Culraick, Murray now acknowledged that it was going to be pretty near impossible to cover the remaining 4 miles before daylight, and even then it was going to take some time to deploy the regiments for their attack.

Murray was talking sense and had just about convinced the others when Colonel Sullivan turned up from the rear with a message from the Prince. The first thing Murray had done when convening his impromptu council of war was send Lochiel back to warn the Prince that the operation might have to be called off. Now, according to Murray, the Irishman responded by pressing him to proceed with the attack, but ultimately left the decision up to his discretion since he 'had the van, and could judge the time'. Sullivan's recollection of the exchange was slightly different and loaded with sufficient incidental detail to be convincing, although the County Kerry man was never one to let facts interfere with a good story, or to pass up an opportunity to needle Murray. As he told this particular story, he began by urging Murray to proceed with the attack:

An interesting picture of a Highlander wearing trews or breeches, and armed with a Turcael or 'Turkish' bladed broadsword.

'Gad Sr,' says Ld George, swearing, 'I desire no better, speak to those gents.' A Colonel of his Regimt [the Atholl Brigade] swore & said if they were to be killed that it would be in plain day, & that they would see how their neighbours would behave ... Another of the Regimt said, 'those that are so much for fighting, why don't they come with us.'

Naturally enough, Sullivan took this as a jibe at staff officers in general and himself in particular, and since the Atholl Brigade had not so far seen any real action, he was having none of it. 'I don't know', says Sullivan:

to whome this discourse is addressed. If it be to me, you know that it was not the first time you saw me in action, you owned it your self & sayed it openly, that you saw no other General but the Prince & me at the battle of Falkirk. If Lord George will permit me, I offer to march in the first rank of his Vanguarde & will give him my head off my shoulders, which is all I have to lose, if he does not succeed, if he follows, & if he follows, I am sure YOU will, Gents.

Happily, the silly squabble was brought to an end by the reappearance of the Duke of Perth and Lord John Drummond, who, like Graden, had been riding down the line, trying to close it up. Now they reported that a huge gap of about half a mile had appeared which would be impossible to close. Whatever Murray's real opinion

Colonel John William Sullivan

Born in County Kerry in 1700, Sullivan was originally destined for the priesthood but instead joined the French Army in 1721. He served under Maréchal Maillebois in Corsica, in Italy and on the Rhine, gaining considerable experience of partisan warfare. By 1745 he was a captain on the General Staff, and on the strength of his experience – and undoubted ability – he was offered a colonel's commission and appointed Prince Charles's chief of staff as both adjutant general and quartermaster general of the Jacobite Army. The stoutly built Irishman clashed almost at once with Lord George Murray, and as the Highland aristocrat came to be regarded as the quintessential hero of the rising, albeit on very shaky grounds, so Sullivan by contrast has all too frequently been cast as an incompetent idiot. In reality, as both his own official account (understandably) and the surviving order books reveal, he was actually a very capable and professional staff officer. Furthermore, since both Murray and the Duke of Perth acted simply as brigade commanders, it was actually Sullivan who exercised operational command of the army at Falkirk and Culloden. Afterwards he was largely responsible for rescuing the Prince and then, with an empty Jacobite knighthood, returned to the French Army and served on the staff at Laffeldt in 1747. Although he was very close to the Prince during the rising, the two men became estranged after Sullivan ran off with Charles's mistress Clementina Walkinshaw.

– and the fact he ordered Graden to remind the men not 'to make any use of our firearms, but only of sword, dirk and bayonet' suggests that initially he may still have been in favour of it – that was sufficient to settle the argument. It was agreed 'upon all hands' that there was now no chance of launching the attack before daylight, although a few took the opportunity to place on record the fact it was not their fault: 'Lochiel and his brother [Dr Archie Cameron] said they had been as much for the night attack as anybody could be, and it was not their fault that it had not been done; but blamed those in the rear that had marched so slow and retarded the rest of the army.' Just at that point John Hay of Restalrig, the Prince's secretary and acting commissary general, turned up with what he supposed was the happy news that the gap in the line had been closed after all, only to be told that everyone had already decided to abandon the attempt. 'He began to argue the point,' sneered Murray, 'but nobody minded him.' That was far from unusual, for by all accounts Restalrig was a weak and ineffectual individual, which is why he no doubt made such a hash of getting supplies brought up the 4 or 5 miles from Inverness to Culloden.

In the circumstances the decision to turn back was undoubtedly the correct one, but it almost resulted in disaster. Murray, having contemptuously dismissed Restalrig, noted that by now it 'was about two o'clock in the morning (the halt not being above a quarter an hour) when they went back in two columns, the rear facing about, and the van taking another way. At a little distance they had a view of the fires of the Duke of Cumberland's camp.' Murray may have been right enough about the time, but his statement that the rear faced about is very wide of the mark.

As he himself admitted, now that it was no longer necessary to conceal his movements, he simply turned off to his left and took his division home by the Church of Croy and the main Inverness road, and thus 'got to Culloden pretty early, so that the men had three or four hours rest'. And much good it would do them, but in the meantime, though Sullivan had agreed to go back and advise the Prince of the change of plan, he and the other messengers failed to find him in the dark and fog. Moreover, contrary to what Restalrig had claimed, the big gap between the front and the rear of the column discovered by Perth had not closed after all, and when Murray turned off to his left, he entirely neglected the elementary but absolutely vital step of leaving a picquet behind to ensure that the other divisions followed suit. The entirely predictable result was that while at least a third of the army was thankfully returning to Culloden, the remainder of the army led by Perth, Drummond and the Prince blithely carried straight on towards Nairn and the British Army.

A local minister named George Innes afterwards claimed they had got the length of Kildrummie, just 2 miles short of their objective, before anyone realized something was amiss. In a memorandum penned rather illiterately in March 1759 the Prince complained that 'he [Murray] turned a crose Rode to retret back, so that Clenronald's Regiment not knowing yet trick advanced ye write rode and came to spake to ye senteris whom he found quite surprised'. Whether Cumberland's sentries or Clanranald's men, confidently assuming the rest of the army was still between them and the enemy, were more surprised is probably a moot point, but having no doubt exchanged the usual pleasantries it was the Jacobites who hastily fell back. 'After we had marched till about three o'clock in the morning, over double the ground that was necessary, we at last came pretty nigh the enemy's camp,' remembered the English Jacobite John Daniel:

> and when we were supposing to surround them, and for that purpose in some measure drawing out; my Lord George Murray began to be missing; notwithstanding the Prince's Aides-de-Camp in riding from rank to rank, and asking, for God's sake! What has become of his Lordship, and telling that the Prince was in the utmost perplexity for want of him. In that situation did we remain a considerable time, till day breaking fast in upon us, we heard that Lord George Murray was gone off with most of the Clans. Where he had been all that considerable time, or what was his intention in it, I leave Time to prove … But O! for Madness!

In fact the Prince was still coming up from the rear when he encountered the Duke of Perth's Regiment heading back towards Culloden, at which point he reportedly called out: 'I am betrayed; what need I give orders, when my orders are disobeyed?' Both Lochiel and Perth also turned up, whereupon Charles demanded to know what was going on. 'What do you mean by ordering the men to turn about?' he expostulated, to which Perth replied that Lord George had turned back three-quarters of an hour before. 'Ld G's vilany proved out of all dispute,' wrote the Prince afterwards, and Clanranald's men no doubt agreed with him. Despite Murray's later elevation to be the quintessential hero of the rebellion by romantic historians, his fellow rebels were generally a good deal less complimentary, and long afterwards, particularly in the MacDonald country, there was a strong tradition that Murray was in fact a traitor.

In the meantime, Lord Elcho, who was presumably present as commander of the Lifeguards, remembered that at first, 'The Prince was not for going back, and said it was much better to march forward and attack, than march back and be attack'd afterwards, when the men would be all fatigued with their night's march. During the time of this Conversation the army, by what means I know not, began to move back.' The Prince, furious, had no alternative but to put a brave face on the situation, and when Perth confirmed that Murray's division was already past recall, he replied, ''Tis no matter then; we shall meet them, and behave like brave fellows.'

And that was the end of it, recalled Elcho, 'and in much shorter time than they had march'd return'd to the parks of Culloden, where Every body seemed to think of nothing but Sleep.' The senior officers at least were lucky enough to find beds in Culloden House, although most made do with tables, chairs and even the floor. Sullivan has a curious tale of how as soon as he got back the Prince confronted Murray 'without the least anger' and demanded to know what had gone wrong, only for Murray to throw 'all the blame on Lochiel', whereupon Lochiel, on being sent for, stoutly asserted it was down to Murray. Although it all sounds most

Another fine study of a Highland gentleman by McIan. Although the hairy sporran may appear anachronistic, at least one example survives from this period.

Although identified by the Penicuik artist as Duncan MacGregor of Dalnasplutrach, the original sketch appears under magnification to be intended as Donald McDonald of Cl—.

unlikely, men are apt to do curious things when asleep on their feet, and, far from being an imaginary encounter as has been suggested, it probably represents a garbled recollection of an incoherent and mutually incomprehensible discussion.

At least, however, someone had the sense to send Fitzjames's Horse back to Inverness to pick up some of the food still waiting there, for without it the army was finished. 'The men were prodigiously tired with hunger and fatigue,' said Elcho, revealing a talent for stating the blindingly obvious, 'and vast numbers of them went to Inverness, and the villages about, both to Sleep and to pick up what little nourishment they Could gett.' One of them was James Johnstone:

> Exhausted with hunger and worn out with the excessive fatigue of the three last nights, as soon as we reached Culloden I turned off as fast as I could for Inverness, where, eager to recruit my strength by a little sleep, I tore off my clothes, half asleep all the while. But when I had already one leg in the bed and was on the point of stretching myself between the sheets, what was my surprise to hear the drum beat to arms and the trumpets of the picket of Fitzjames sounding the call to boot and saddle. I hurried on my clothes, my eyes half shut, and mounting a horse, instantly repaired to our army on the eminence on which we had remained for three days, and from which we now saw the English army at a distance of about two miles from us.

Just as they had done on the previous day, the Jacobites drew up in order of battle on the moor, but with neither the same numbers nor the same fragile confidence, and long before the British Army arrived they were in trouble. In the first place large numbers of men, like Johnstone, had dispersed in search of food, and did not always have the same sense of duty (or the horse) that carried him back as the crisis approached. Moreover, the countryside between Nairn and Inverness was also littered with exhausted stragglers from the night march, soundly sleeping in ditches and under bushes and walls, as well as in every convenient house, byre and stable for miles around. The entirely predictable result was that far from drawing up in a proper soldier-like fashion, the rebels were simply standing about in untidy clumps up and down the moor, with the colours of each regiment in more or less the right place, but large gaps between them as they waited for the men to come in, singly or even by whole companies. And even while they waited, the officers wrangled among themselves.

CHAPTER IV

High Noon on a Blasted Heath

O stensibly the argument was over a matter of precedence. Almost from the very beginning of the campaign the rebels had paid lip-service to a policy of rotating units through the post of honour in the van. In theory too the regiment supposedly leading the army on the march would also occupy the very right of the line in the event that there should be a battle that day. In practice, of course, a physical rotation of this kind would have played havoc with the army's tactical command structure by switching units between divisions according to the day of the week, and instead honour was usually satisfied all round by passing the Prince's own standard to a different unit each day, while in both previous battles Perth's MacDonalds division had claimed the right wing on the strength of a tradition stretching back to Robert the Bruce's day. It was not quite in accordance with the theory, but it worked – until 15 April.

Up to that point the three battalion strong Atholl Brigade, though recruited in the Perthshire glens, had always been reckoned as a Lowland unit. Strictly speaking a great many of the men serving in its ranks were actually Highlanders, of course, but it was widely acknowledged that they were not to be regarded socially or militarily in quite the same light as the 'wilder' clansmen from the north and west of the Great Glen. At both Prestonpans and Falkirk, therefore, the Atholl Brigade marched in the second line, as part of the reserve. Now, however, perhaps stung by unkind aspersions that 'There was not an officer or soldier of them killed or wounded since the beginning of the Campagne', Lord George Murray had insisted they should have the right of the front line. 'The McDonnells had the left that day,' complained Donald McDonnell of Lochgarry, who had commanded Glengarry's Regiment since Falkirk:

> the Prince having agreed to give the right to Ld George and his Atholemen. Upon which Clanranald, Keppoch and I spoke to his RHs upon that subject, and begg'd he wou'd allow us our former right, but he intreated us for his sake we wou'd not dispute it, as he had already agreed to give it to Lord George and

his Atholemen; and I heard HRHs say that he resented it much, and should never doe the like if he had occasion for it. Your Regt. That I had the honr to command at the battle was about 500 strong, and that same day your people of Glenmoriston were on the way to join us, on the other side of Lochness.

The letter is slightly confusing in that although on first reading Lochgarry appears to be talking about something which happened on the morning of 16 April, he was actually discussing the initial decision to grant the right to the Athollmen the previous day. And so Murray's men stood on the right of the front line throughout that long day and then led the night march, while the MacDonalds marched in the rear of the army and eventually stumbled on into Cumberland's picquet line after Murray went home without telling anybody.

Now the Athollmen, better rested than anyone else in the army, were still standing on the right when the army drew up again on the morning of 16 April, and the argument was about to resurface – in a surprisingly different form. In the meantime, Lochgarry and everyone else had a more immediate problem. In condemning the choice of Culloden Moor as a battlefield, critics have almost invariably overlooked the fact that the ground originally reconnoitred and chosen by Sullivan, in his dual capacity of adjutant general and quartermaster general, was *not* the ground on which the battle was eventually fought. The original concentration area chosen by Sullivan, where the army awaited Cumberland during the daylight hours of 15 April and the morning of 16 April, was actually the flat expanse of moorland at round about NH4575 on the Ordnance Survey map. However, that morning it soon became all too clear that hundreds of men were still missing after the disastrous

The famous Laurie and Whittle print of the Battle of Culloden is a grand collage representing its various incidents rather than a single snapshot picture.

Culloden Moor, looking towards the Jacobite lines, marked by the fringe of trees along the horizon.

march, and indeed one account comments that the so-called battle line consisted of nothing more substantial than scattered groups of men clustered around their colours. Recognizing that they still had insufficient men present to fight on that particular ground, the rebels therefore fell back and, according to Harry Ker of Graden (who as an engineer should have known what he was talking about), took up a new position 'a mile westward' of their original one.

In all the circumstances this new and hastily chosen battlefield was probably making the best of a bad job. Lying on top of a broad ridge running approximately from east to west, the battlefield can be considered with some justification to be just the eastern extremity of the much larger Drummossie Moor, which provides the fight with its alternative name. The actual land on which the battle was fought, however, formed and largely still does form a part of the Culloden estate, and so the more familiar name is certainly the correct one. In 1746 the moor was a comparatively level, if uneven, stretch of grassy 'outfield' or common grazing land used by the surrounding tenant farmers. It was flanked on one side, the south-east, by a fairly steep slope running down to the Water of Nairn, and on the north-west by a slightly shallower slope down to Culloden House and the main road to Inverness. Although the moor itself was wide open, the slopes on either side were put down partly to open fields cultivated by the still current runrig (or strip) system, and partly to 'infields' enclosed by substantial drystone walls. These walls meant that the Jacobite position was difficult to outflank. In the event Cumberland was able to pass most of his cavalry around the side of the rebel army, but that was a tactical move during the battle itself. In advancing to contact he had no alternative but to march straight at the Jacobites on their own ground.

Culloden Moor, looking towards the modern Culchunaig. The Atholl Brigade advanced over this ground towards camera.

While generally level in appearance (and perhaps even looking disappointingly flat to the visitor), that ground actually falls by approximately 10 metres in height over the 500 metres separating the initial position of the Jacobite right wing, anchored on some walls by the farmstead of Culchunaig, and the ground where Barrell's 4th Foot would stand just forward of another farmstead at Leanach. There is also a similar fall of about 20 metres over the 1,100 metres separating the Jacobite

Culloden Moor as viewed from the position occupied by Barrell's Regiment, looking out over the wet dip created by the Well of the Dead, which formed a final obstacle to the Jacobite advance.

Front view of Old Leanach cottage, Culloden Moor. It was once touted as a survivor of the battle, but estate records and archaeological investigations have established that the original was first rebuilt in about 1760 and then 'restored' to its present state in about 1881.

right from the extreme left wing, similarly anchored on the Culloden park walls on the other side of the battlefield. Slashing diagonally across the moorland between the two armies was an unmetalled road, the precursor of the modern B9006. Of itself it would have no real tactical significance except for the very important fact that it seems to have marked the boundary between a relatively dry and flat area on the very top of the moor to the south of the road, and the very noticeably lower and wetter ground to the north of the road. In fact, like much of upland Scotland, the soil of the moor itself was too thin to absorb the abundant winter rain and too flat to allow it to run off easily. Consequently, though covered with rough grass rather than heather, it was and to some extent still is at best very wet and spewy ground with a number of springs or 'wells', and in some places is downright boggy.

Because the area about to be fought over was relatively intensely farmed there were also a number of buildings scattered across it; some had no tactical significance at all, but the principal ones belonged to the two farmsteads at Leanach and Culchunaig. The former is currently represented by a single cottage once believed to be a survivor of the battle, but now known to have been built in about 1881, and the latter by some unequivocally late nineteenth- or early twentieth-century farm buildings. Although both steadings now provide useful reference points, the available documentary and archaeological evidence – and in particular Thomas Sandby's maps and sketches – indicates that while the present Leanach cottage occupies the footprints of the original turf-walled building, the modern Culchunaig may be nearer to the Culwhiniac walls than was the original.

Rear view of Old Leanach cottage, Culloden Moor. Although no physical trace of the 1746 structure remains above ground, archaeological investigation has established that the present building occupies the original footprint.

The rebel army eventually formed up on the moor facing to the north-east, with its left wing resting on the south-eastern corner of a series of drystone-walled enclosures known as the Culloden Parks, being part of the Mains or home farm attached to Culloden House, which lay at the bottom of the long, shallow slope stretching down from the moor towards the main Inverness road and the Moray Firth. These walls provided a secure anchor point for the left flank, but forward of this point the moor was wide open. On the other hand it was boggy enough to inhibit movement, especially by horsemen – and in some places soldiers on both sides would find themselves knee-deep in water. The moor was rather drier on the other side, near Culchunaig, where the Jacobite right wing was anchored on the extreme western corner of the stone-walled Culwhiniac enclosures. These stretched (and still do stretch) all the way down to the Water of Nairn. Forward of these particular stone walls a horseshoe-shaped turf-walled enclosure bulged out onto the moor beside the farm at Leanach.

When Murray complained to Sullivan that this particular ground had not been reconnoitred, which was hardly surprising in the circumstances, the Adjutant General responded that:

> here is as good a position as you could desire. You see that Park before you which continues to the river with a wall six foot high, & them houses near it, which you can fill with men, & pierce the walls, that is on your right. You see

this Park here is to be our left, & both in a direct line. If there be not ground enough, we'll make use of the Parks & I'll warrant you My Lord, says Sullivan, the horse won't come to you there. He [Murray] went off grumbling.

In contrast to the rather precipitate way in which both sides set about each other in the two earlier battles, Culloden was characterized by a slow and deliberate build-up and a considerable amount of jockeying for position. If Sullivan is to be believed, the exchange just recounted followed directly on from a complaint by Murray that his Athollmen were still standing on the right:

> Lord George comes up and tells Sullivan who had the honr to be near the Prince, that he must change the order of battle, that his Regimt had the right yesterday. 'But My Lord,' says Sullivan, 'there was no battle yesterday, besides it is no time to change the order of battle in the enemy's presence.' 'Lead up the men then, [says Murray,] its your business to set them in battle.' 'That I will My Lord,' says Sullivan. 'If you'll be so good as to make them follow in their ranks, that there may be more confusion, for there is nothing more dangerous than to change Regimts from one ground to another in the presence of the enemy.' The Prince caressed Lord George, prayed him to lead the men, and that he and Sullivan would make them follow in their ranks. 'Gad Sir,' says Lord George swearing, 'it is hard that my Regimt must have the right two days running' when it is he himself would have it so absolutely.

The language is a touch confused but it seems clear that as the army started to take up its new position on the moor between the Culwhiniac enclosures and the Culloden Parks, Murray attempted to have his men moved from the right wing into a different position. Just where that position might have been is not stated, but the resulting gap would need to be filled, and if the MacDonalds were to claim the post instead, then, as Sullivan correctly pointed out, it would result in the army completely changing its order of battle in the presence of the enemy. Matters were confused enough already without that.

As it was, then, the Jacobite front line originally comprised: 3 battalions of the Atholl Brigade on the extreme right, totalling about 500 men; Lochiel's 650 Camerons; Charles Stewart of Ardsheal's 150 strong Appin Battalion; Lieutenant Colonel Charles Fraser of Inverallochy's battalion of Lovat's Regiment, mustering about 500 men (the other battalion, commanded by the Master of Lovat, was still hurrying towards the battlefield); then Lady Mackintosh's 500 men under Lieutenant Colonel Alexander McGillivray of Dunmaglas; Francis Farquharson of Monaltrie's 150 men from Deeside; then a small combined battalion of MacLeans and MacLachlans and a little contingent of Chisholms, all 3 of whom totalled no more than about 280 men; and finally 3 MacDonald battalions commanded by Keppoch, Clanranald and Lochgarry respectively, of whom the first 2 mustered about 200 men apiece, while Lochgarry, by his own testimony, had as many as 500. In total, therefore, there should have been something like 3,630 men in the front line, besides officers and volunteers, but all accounts agree that their ranks were severely depleted by straggling, and that there may in fact have been several hundred fewer at the start of the battle. At any rate, assuming that all were drawn up 4 deep in accordance with French tactical doctrine (see Chapter 7) and allowing the necessary 1 metre per file, this would produce a notional frontage of some 900 metres, and by the time the necessary intervals between each battalion are factored in, the whole lot will have fitted very comfortably into the 1,100 metre gap between the Culwhiniac and Culloden park walls.

Behind them there was no fully formed second line as such. Instead, drawing on the experience of Falkirk, the Jacobites instead simply had a number of units scattered along the rear of the first and deployed in column rather than line in order to act as mobile reserves, in accordance with French tactical doctrine. Again, working from right to left, there were the regular Royal Ecossois, commanded by Lord Lewis Drummond and numbering as many as 350 men, posted in the rear of Murray's division. Next, more or less in the centre, came the main 'reserve' under Colonel John Roy Stuart, comprising 2 battalions of Lord Lewis Gordon's Aberdeenshire Regiment, commanded by John Gordon of Avochie and James Moir of Stonywood respectively, the first being about 300 strong and the latter having around 200 men; then two battalions of Lord Ogilvy's Forfarshire Regiment, mustering another 500 between them; John Roy Stuart's Regiment, numbering about 200; Lord Kilmarnock's Footguards, probably commanded by James Crichton of Auchengoul, with another 200; old John Gordon of Glenbuchat's Regiment with the same; and the Duke of Perth's Regiment, commanded by the Master of Strathallan with 300. Finally, mirroring the deployment of the Royal Ecossois on the right, the left flank of the second line was covered by the regular Irish Picquets commanded by Lieutenant Colonel Walter Stapleton. This composite battalion comprised detachments from the French army's Irish regiments: Dillon, Rooth, Lally and Berwick, and no doubt some dismounted troopers of Fitzjames's Cavalerie, making a combined total of some 300 men. Once again, however, it has to be stressed that, with the likely exception of the two 'French' units, these various figures represent the estimated strength of each unit on 15 April and that the actual numbers standing on the moor at the outset of the battle next day may have been appreciably less.

Further back still were three bodies of cavalry: firstly a composite squadron made up of Lord Elcho's Lifeguards and part of the regular Irish regiment Fitzjames's Cavalerie on the right, while another combined squadron collectively referred to as the 'Highland Horse', formed from Bagot's Hussars, Lord Strathallan's Horse and perhaps some of Balmerino's Lifeguards, was on the left. Finally a small escort troop of Lifeguards and Fitzjames's Cavalerie stood with the Prince in the centre. The latter group numbered just sixteen men, while the two others seem to have numbered no more than about seventy apiece. All of them, it should be noted, were mounted, however badly. Popular legend notwithstanding, there were no pathetic huddles of dismounted cavalrymen standing aimlessly in the rear. Instead, those individual troopers lacking horses for whatever reason were either incorporated into the ranks of Lord Kilmarnock's Footguards, or else standing in other infantry regiments of their choice.

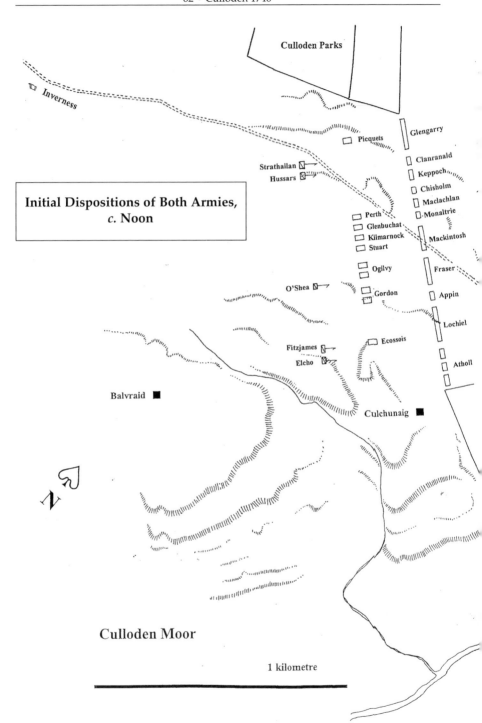

Culloden Parks

Inverness

Glengarry

Picquets

Clanranald

Strathallan

Keppoch

Hussars

Chisholm

Maclachlan

Perth

Monaltrie

Glenbuchat

Kilmarnock

Mackintosh

Stuart

Ogilvy

Fraser

O'Shea

Gordon

Appin

Lochiel

Ecossois

Fitzjames

Elcho

Atholl

Balvraid

Culchunaig

N

**Initial Dispositions of Both Armies,
c. Noon**

Culloden Moor

1 kilometre

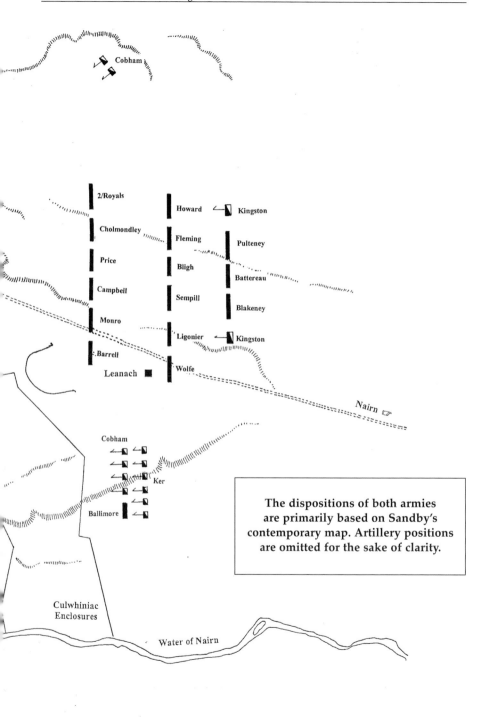

Cobham

2/Royals

Howard ← Kingston

Cholmondley

Fleming

Pulteney

Price

Bligh

Battereau

Campbell

Sempill

Blakeney

Monro

Ligonier ← Kingston

Barrell

Leanach ■

Wolfe

Nairn ☞

Cobham

← ←
← ←
← ←
← ← Ker
←
Ballimore ←

The dispositions of both armies
are primarily based on Sandby's
contemporary map. Artillery positions
are omitted for the sake of clarity.

Culwhiniac
Enclosures

Water of Nairn

Where the British Army Came From

It is now widely recognized that the Duke of Cumberland commanded a British army rather than an English one at Culloden. In fact, four out of his sixteen infantry battalion were Scottish units: the Royals (now better known as the Royal Scots), Campbell's Royal Scots Fusiliers, Sempill's 'Edinburgh Regiment' (later the King's Own Scottish Borderers) and of course a Highland battalion, commonly known as the Argyle Militia, which included elements of both the regular 64th Highlanders and even some officers and a cadre of the 43rd/42nd Black Watch. In addition to these units, which all had depot companies in Scotland at the outset of the rising, other regiments in Cumberland's army also had substantial numbers of Scots serving in their ranks. In 1740, for example, over a third of the officers in Pulteney's 13th Foot were Scots, and as such will have done most of their recruiting north of the border to produce a similar proportion in the rank and file. Similarly Ker's 11th Dragoons were originally raised as a Scottish regiment and still had a large number of Scottish officers at Culloden, as indeed did Captain Godwin's artillery company.

Although it would be quite wrong to refer to Cumberland's army as the Hanoverian army, there was, oddly enough, a small unit present from that army – the Duke's personal bodyguard of hussars.

As the rebels gathered up on the moor, the British Army advanced towards them in four columns, preceded by a composite Highland battalion, made up of elements of both the regular 43rd/42nd Highlanders (the Black Watch) and 64th Highlanders, as well as by the loyalist Argyle Militia. Three of the columns comprised five infantry battalions formed in line and ranked one behind the other, while the fourth comprised all three regiments of cavalry. Requiring the infantry battalions to march a long distance in line must have considerably slowed Cumberland's approach, but no one was in any doubt that they were advancing to contact and might find themselves in action at any time. To

Highland soldiers in the British Army. The figure on the right is identified as a corporal by the knotted cord on his right shoulder – a symbolic representation of the skein of slow match carried by corporals in the days when their men were armed with matchlocks.

deploy into order of battle the second and fourth battalions in each column needed only to move out to their left and then forward into the gaps between the first and third battalions. By this simple means it was possible to form very quickly two lines each of six battalions, and a reserve of three battalions, and the deployment was rehearsed immediately on leaving Nairn and again as soon as the rebel army was sighted. However, when the Jacobites showed no signs of coming forward to meet them, the army formed its columns once again and advanced up the moor as far as Leanach, where Cumberland deployed for the last time and now brought his guns up as well.

In contrast to the loose estimates available for most of the Jacobite units, a morning state survives for Cumberland's army which provides very precise figures for those present that day. Initially his front line, commanded by the Earl of Albemarle, comprised the 1st and 3rd Brigades. From right (i.e. directly opposite the MacDonalds) to left were: 2/1st (Royal) Regiment with 26 officers, 29 sergeants, 25 drummers and 401 rank and file; then Cholmondley's 34th Foot with 24 officers, 21 sergeants, 15 drums and 399 men; and Price's 14th Foot mustering 23 officers, 21 sergeants, 11 drums and 304 men. Next came the 21st (Royal Scots Fusiliers) with 19 officers, 21 sergeants, 14 drums and 358 men; Monro's 37th Foot, which was the strongest battalion on the field, with 23 officers, 23 sergeants, 19 drums and 426 men; and finally Barrell's 4th Foot, which, with 20 officers, 18 sergeants, 10 drums and just 325 men, was one of the smallest.

Between each of the battalions in the front line was a little Royal Artillery detachment, manning two 3 lb cannon apiece, and there were also two batteries each

of three Coehorn mortars at the ends of the second line, the whole lot being manned by 10 officers and 106 gunners under the immediate command of Captain Lieutenant John Godwin. Lieutenant Colonel William Belford, the man normally credited with commanding Cumberland's gunners, actually held a staff appointment as Commander Royal Artillery (CRA), and as such was primarily responsible for the administration of the artillery train and the army's ammunition columns, rather than the immediate tactical control of the guns.

Cumberland's second line, commanded by Major General John Huske, was originally made up of the 2nd and 4th Brigades. These, again from right to left, comprised: Howard's 3rd (Buffs) with 16 officers, 21 sergeants, 14 drummers and 413 rank and file; Fleming's 36th Foot with 26 officers, 25 sergeants, 14 drummers and 350 men; Bligh's 20th Foot with 20 officers, 22 sergeants, 13 drummers and 412 men; then Sempill's 25th (Edinburgh) Regiment mustering 23 officers, 20 sergeants, 14 drummers and 420 men;

An officer of the Royal Artillery, c. 1742.

Ligonier's 59th/48th Foot with 24 officers,
21 sergeants, 16 drummers and 325 men;
and finally Edward Wolfe's 8th Foot with
22 officers, 17 sergeants, 11 drums and 324 rank
and file. Blindly perpetuating an error in John
Home's *History of the Rebellion* published in 1802,
most modern accounts of the battle erroneously
depict the 8th Foot taking up a rather improbable
position forward of and at a right angle to Barrell's 4th
Foot on the left of the front line. In reality, as we shall see
in the next chapter, it remained in the second line until
ordered forward during the decisive counter-attack.

The third line or reserve comprised Brigadier
Mordaunt's 5th Brigade, that is to say: Pulteney's
13th Foot with 22 officers, 23 sergeants, 19 drums and
410 men; Battereau's 62nd Foot with 27 officers,
24 sergeants, 18 drums and 354 men; and finally
Blakeney's 27th Foot, which had 20 officers, 24 sergeants,
12 drummers and 300 rank and file. Flanking this
brigade were both squadrons of Kingston's 10th
Horse, totalling 211 officers and men.

The rest of the cavalry comprised two dragoon
regiments (less one squadron which was off
reconnoitring to the north) under Major General
Humphrey Bland. These were posted on the left of
the line, not with anything clever in mind, but simply
because it appeared to be the only ground dry
enough for them. Cobham's 10th Dragoons had 276 officers and men present that
morning, of whom about 90 were detached on reconnaissance, while Ker's had about

This soldier of Pulteney's 13th Foot was sketched some years after the battle, but nevertheless provides a good picture of a typical British infantryman.

A group of Highland clansmen about to engage dragoons.

300. Once in contact with the enemy the Highland battalion was under orders to retire to the baggage train, not through any doubts as to their proven reliability, but rather to avoid any friendly-fire incidents. While some of the regulars belonging to the 43rd/42nd Highlanders and 64th Highlanders obviously had red jackets, the Argyle Militia had no uniform at all, and after Falkirk there was even a serious suggestion that they should be issued with soldiers' hats instead of bonnets in order to readily distinguish them from the rebels. In the event nothing came of this intriguing idea, but while one wing of the battalion, commanded by Lieutenant Colonel Jack Campbell of Mamore, duly fell back to the rear, the other, led by another 64th officer, Captain Colin Campbell of Ballimore, remained with the Dragoons. There were four companies in this half-battalion, a regular company of the 64th under Ballimore himself and another of the 43rd under Captain Dugald Campbell of Auchrossan, and two companies of the Argyle Militia led by John Campbell of Achnaba and a Captain Duncan Campbell. One account speaks of there being 140 of them, but it is unclear whether this refers to the 2 militia companies only or includes the regulars; it is possible that there could well have been 200 officers and men in total. At any event, while they were clearly the smallest of Cumberland's infantry units, they were still the equal in numbers of many Jacobite units.

Ahead of him General Bland could see the stone walls of the Culwhiniac enclosures, and he had a shrewd idea that if he were to get his cavalry brigade through them he ought to be able to turn the rebels' flank. In order to do that, however, he needed infantry support. Cumberland's second in command, Lieutenant General Henry Hawley, agreed, and so instead of retiring to the baggage train, Ballimore's Highlanders were sent forward to tear gaps in the walls.

In the meantime the rebels were not standing still either. As we have seen, Sullivan anchored the flanks of the front line on the corners of the Culloden and Culwhiniac parks, but Lord George Murray, who commanded the right wing, became increasingly concerned about the obstacle which the protruding Leanach enclosure would create for any attack. Eventually, he unilaterally advanced his men down the moor, apparently to a gateway about halfway along the western wall of the Culwhiniac enclosures, and once there he formed the three battalions of the Atholl Brigade into columns in order to better manoeuvre around the Leanach wall when the attack actually began. Although this move was sensible enough in itself, it was carried out without prior consultation and resulted in some considerable dislocation on both sides.

In the first place it appears to have taken the Jacobite left wing by surprise for it was at this time, rather than later, that the MacDonalds famously refused, despite the urgings of the Duke of Perth, to conform by moving forward. This was hardly surprising, since it very obviously meant they would give up the security of the park walls and be left with their flank standing dangerously in the air. The immediate consequence was that since the left wing remained anchored on the corner of the Culloden walls, the line now stretched along a rather greater frontage and large gaps now appeared. To his astonishment Colonel Sullivan heard cries of 'Close, close!' and found 'intervals, that he had not seen before'. In the circumstances there was no alternative but to turn to the second line, 'for there was no time to be lost, to fill up the vacancy that was left (by Ld George's changement)'. Sullivan later recalled that he brought forward Perth's and Strathallan's regiments,

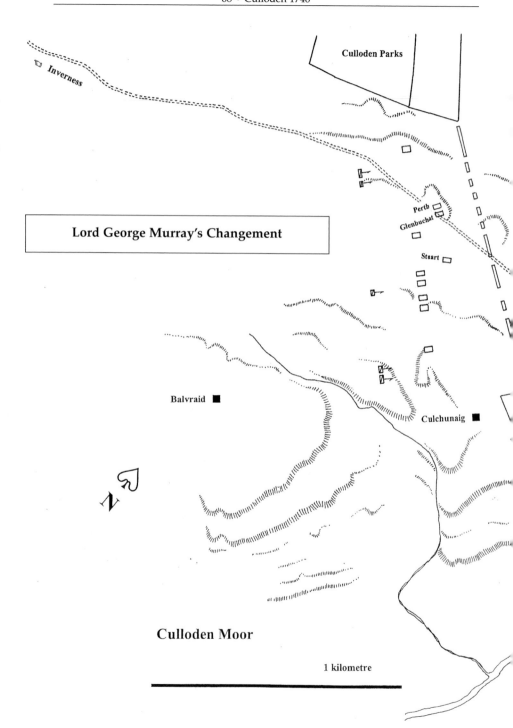

Culloden Parks

Lord George Murray's Changement

Inverness

Perth

Glenbuchat

Stuart

Balvraid ■

Culchunaig ■

N

Culloden Moor

1 kilometre

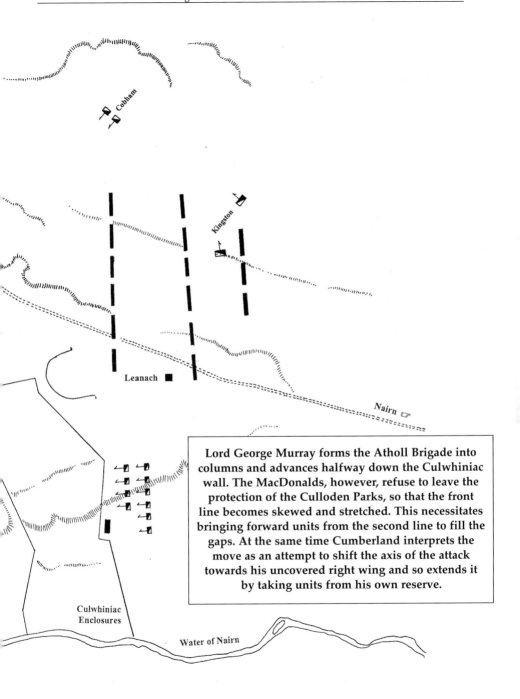

Cobham

Kingston

Leanach

Nairn ☞

Lord George Murray forms the Atholl Brigade into columns and advances halfway down the Culwhiniac wall. The MacDonalds, however, refuse to leave the protection of the Culloden Parks, so that the front line becomes skewed and stretched. This necessitates bringing forward units from the second line to fill the gaps. At the same time Cumberland interprets the move as an attempt to shift the axis of the attack towards his uncovered right wing and so extends it by taking units from his own reserve.

Culwhiniac
Enclosures

Water of Nairn

but must have been confused by the fact that Perth's Regiment was actually commanded by the Master of Strathallan, for by the time his redeployment was complete it was Perth's and Glenbuchat's regiments that stood on the extreme left of the front line instead of the MacDonalds, who 'by this had no more the left, they were almost in the Center', and John Roy Stuart's Regiment had also been sent forward into the middle of the line to stand beside Stewart of Ardsheal's men. These additions increased the strength of the front line to a total of around 4,430 men, although it once again needs to be emphasized that this is still an estimate which takes no account of the previous day's straggling.

The move also resulted in some problems for the Jacobite gunners. At the outset of the battle they had 11 guns emplaced just forward of their front line. Most Jacobite maps show them deployed in three batteries on the flanks and centre, but Paul Sandby, a draughtsman on Cumberland's staff, afterwards depicted a group of four on the right in front of the Atholl Brigade, two in front of John Roy Stuart's Regiment, three in front of Lady Mackintosh's Regiment and the remaining two guns in front of the MacLeans and MacLachlans. The obvious conclusion, of course, is that they were initially placed neatly enough in three batteries but became scattered when the line moved and shifted during Lord George Murray's 'changement' (Map 3, pp. 68–9). It may be as well to mention at this point that all of them were evidently 3-pounders, and there is absolutely no foundation for modern suggestions that their efficiency was impaired by the need to service a multiplicity of calibres. The rebels did indeed have a wide and varied selection of cannon, but all but one of those firing non-standard ammunition were left behind either at Inverness or at Culloden House. The sole exception was a twelfth gun brought up by a French engineer officer, Captain Du Saussey, after the battle had started. This was almost certainly a 4-pounder, but he was evidently sensible enough to bring a sufficient quantity of the right ammunition with him.

All of this shifting about did not go unnoticed by the Duke of Cumberland, although it is hardly surprising that in the circumstances he evidently misinterpreted its significance. The reshuffling of individual units aside, the end result of the 'changement' was that the Jacobite front line had in effect wheeled slightly to its left and so to all appearances had shifted the axis of its advance more towards the north. In practical terms this suggested that the main weight of the rebel attack would fall on Cumberland's open right flank, which was already to some extent 'outwinged'. He in turn responded, therefore, by posting himself on the right of the 2nd Battalion of the Royals and bringing forward two of Mordaunt's battalions from the third line – Pulteney's 13th Foot and Battereau's 62nd Foot – to prolong the right of his first and second lines respectively. At the same time both squadrons of Kingston's 10th Horse were also brought forward from the reserve to cover the right flank and were then joined there by two troops of Cobham's 10th Dragoons who had earlier been sent reconnoitring towards the north. The end result was that Cumberland's front line now numbered exactly 2,623 bayonets under 461 officers and NCOs, plus about 300 cavalrymen.

On paper it was significantly outnumbered by the rebels.

CHAPTER V

Claymore!

M eanwhile, General Hawley had begun moving through the Culwhiniac enclosures in order to try to outflank the rebels. This move had been anticipated by the Jacobites and led to another acrimonious exchange between Sullivan and Murray. The former was encouragingly dismissive of the danger at first, but nevertheless recommended that 'as all their horse is at their left, that we shou'd make a breach in this wall, & set in this park Stonywood & the other Regiment [Avochie's] that is in Colloum behind you, who will take their horse in flank, without fearing in the least that they can come upon him.' Predictably, Murray ignored this suggestion on principle, and George Innes reported that: 'Some of Stoniewood's regiment assert, that Colonel Baggot had advised to post them along the outside of that park-dyke, which probably would have prevented a good deal of the mischief these Campbells and dragoons afterwards did; but that Lord George Murray would not hear of it.' Instead Sullivan (not Bagot) posted them in a 'hollow way' near Culchunaig, after enjoining Stonywood to keep a sentry posted on top to warn of any approaching trouble.

Entirely predictably this meant that Hawley and his men were able to traverse the enclosure 'without receiving one shot from the two battalions that were placed to observe their motions'. On the other hand, though they might certainly have harassed the dragoons as they rode past, and could certainly have stopped Ballimore's men seizing control of the upper part of the enclosure, it was on balance just as well that they did not post themselves inside, for it seems doubtful that a defensive line could have been cobbled together to stop Hawley on the other side of Culchunaig without them. Locating the position of that defensive line is important for it widens out the battlefield considerably. There is general agreement that the rebels and the dragoons eventually faced each other over a feature variously described as a 'hollow way', a 'ditch' and even in some secondary sources as a 'sunken road'. This is often identified as the deep hollow bending around the north and east sides of the present Culchunaig steading. Even a cursory examination of the ground, however, will demonstrate that this particular hollow allows a frontage of only about 100 metres between the steading and the Culwhiniac walls, which is barely enough to accommodate a single squadron of cavalry, let alone the formidable concentration which was building up on both sides. Sandby, it is true, certainly appears to depict the dragoons partly facing a cluster of buildings obviously intended to represent Culchunaig, but a closer examination of both his maps and an ink-wash sketch which he produced of the battle reveals that not only was the original steading probably further to the west of the present buildings, but that in any case most of the dragoons were further west still. Indeed, Captain Duncan Campbell of the Argyles stated that 'The Dragoons went out and formed at a distance, facing the rebels,' while Lord Elcho even more explicitly described the position taken up by his regiment as 'a ditch which Cover'd the right wing' – which clearly establishes it as a much more substantial feature than the hollow by Culchunaig.

Instead, as the dragoons cleared the parks they swung around to deploy into two lines on the open slope below a much longer re-entrant which runs for about 500 metres more or less in a straight line from west to east on the other side of Culchunaig. To all intents and purposes Hawley was not on the rebel flank but their rear. All too aware of the danger further Jacobite reinforcements were hurried over to it, and by the time Hawley actually closed up to the re-entrant, the crest above was lined by a total of four battalions from Lord Lewis Gordon's and Lord Ogilvy's regiments, and the combined squadron of Fitzjames's Horse and Elcho's Lifeguards.

Unsurprisingly, being unable to see anything of what lay behind the crest and perhaps unaware of his opportunity, Hawley declined to force a passage across the

Culchunaig as seen from the Culwhiniac wall a little way above the site of the breach. The depression which can been seen between the farm and the wall, sometimes referred to as a sunken road, provided shelter for Moir of Stonywood's battalion at one point during the battle.

The re-entrant west of Culchunaig which held up the advance of Hawley and his dragoons.

re-entrant and instead settled down to await events. One of Hawley's staff officers, Major James Wolfe – the future conqueror of Quebec – recorded that the firing began at one o'clock in the afternoon. Other eyewitnesses thought it began earlier, but although there was to be no real consensus on the hour there was universal agreement that the cannonade was opened by the rebels – and probably in response to the realization that Hawley's cavalry was in the army's rear.

The Jacobite gunnery is usually claimed to have been totally ineffective, and an analysis of British casualty returns suggests that the Jacobite guns killed or wounded only about twenty officers and men. The Royal Artillery by contrast was rather more efficient, although its effectiveness has just as consistently been overstated. After the Jacobites had fired just twice in a ripple across their front,

The re-entrant was not a significant obstacle in itself but as this photograph clearly shows, the higher ground, which was lined with Jacobites, prevented Hawley from seeing what lay beyond.

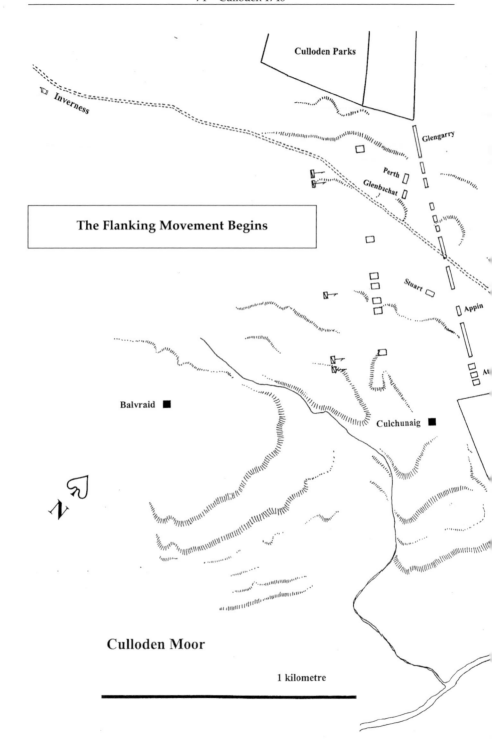

Culloden Parks

Inverness

Glengarry

Perth

Glenbachat

The Flanking Movement Begins

Stuart

Appin

Balvraid

Culchunaig

N

Culloden Moor

1 kilometre

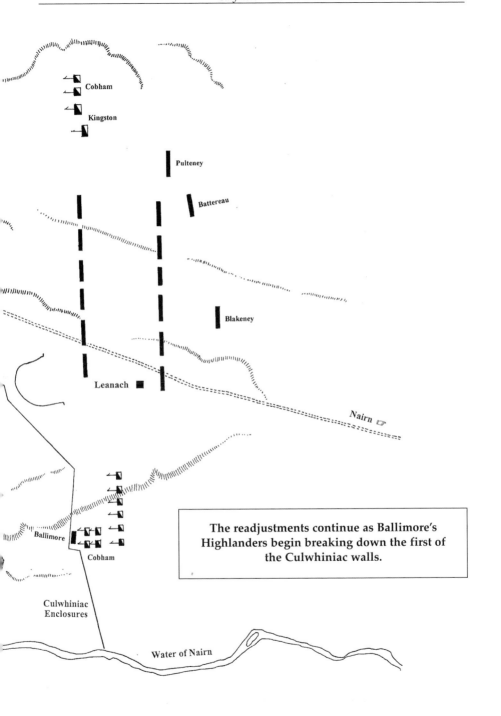

Cobham

Kingston

Pulteney

Battereau

Blakeney

Leanach

Nairn

Ballimore

Cobham

The readjustments continue as Ballimore's Highlanders begin breaking down the first of the Culwhiniac walls.

Culwhiniac
Enclosures

Water of Nairn

Captain Godwin's ten guns replied. Exaggerated accounts reaching Edinburgh only a few days later claimed that the British Army's bombardment went on for over an hour before the clansmen commenced their attack, but this is palpable nonsense. Perceptions of time under fire are always subjective, but Jacobite accounts suggesting that they were fired upon for between 20 and 30 minutes have been uncritically accepted by most historians. In practical terms, however, an artillery preparation of such a comparatively lengthy duration would have severely depleted the ammunition actually up with the guns (the usual ammunition scale at this time was forty rounds apiece, including the reserve in the park), and by contrast the British accounts all record a much shorter bombardment. James Wolfe reckoned it lasted 15 minutes, but as he was unable actually to see what was going on he was relying on sound alone, and his estimate must relate to the whole period between the first of the Jacobite guns opening fire and then the last of the British ones ceasing fire because the cavalry were going forward. Similarly, back with the baggage train Campbell of Airds put its total duration at a very precise 9 minutes, but those in a position to actually see what was happening told of an even briefer exchange still. Indeed, one of Cumberland's ADCs, Joseph Yorke, wrote to his father that: 'When our cannon had fired about two rounds, I could plainly perceive that the rebels fluctuated extremely, and could not remain long in the position they were then in without running away or coming down upon us; and according as I thought, in two or three minutes they broke from the centre in three large bodies.' On balance, therefore, Airds's estimate is most likely to be correct, since it must include both the initial exchange of fire and then the firing up to the point when the charging Highlanders came within musket range.

Over those 9 minutes Godwin's men are unlikely to have fired more than a total of 90 rounds, most of them at extreme range. It was rare for cannonballs to strike directly onto their intended target, and gunners usually preferred to drop them short and let them skip along until they hit something useful. However, at Culloden the soft ground will have adversely affected that 'grazing' or skipping effect which kept the balls moving just above ground level, while conversely there is ample testimony that a significant number of rounds went over the front line to come down – usually harmlessly – in the rear. Taking these factors into account along with statistical analysis of contemporary gunnery tests, it is unlikely that Godwin succeeded in killing or wounding more than an average of one man per shot fired. In other words the supposed holocaust described by all too many modern writers probably amounted to no more than 90 to 100 killed or wounded in total – a long way from the third or more of the rebel strength postulated by some.

Nevertheless, to men unused to artillery fire it was still more than enough, and they became increasing impatient at the apparent lack of action by their commanders. The widespread but quite erroneous belief that the British artillery preparation lasted for half an hour or more has in turn spawned another set of myths and legends as to why the order to begin the charge was delayed for so long. An arrogant and uncaring Prince is frequently pictured sitting on his horse far in the rear, oblivious to the carnage being wrought on his men while message after frantic message is sent back begging for permission to attack. In point of fact he himself had been demanding that his men go forward even before they were properly formed. It is clear, however, that the straggling which resulted from the disastrous night march was so bad that men were still rejoining their units after the battle began, and it was not just individuals who were missing. Whole companies and at least one complete regiment were also known to be hurrying towards the battlefield and likely to arrive at any moment. There were therefore sound reasons for delaying attacking for as long as possible, right up until the moment Hawley's cavalry came through the Culwhiniac enclosure and the guns started firing. Once that did happen, judging by the various timings offered by British officers, it is quite clear that if there was a further delay, it was of no more than 5 minutes after the cannonade began. Moreover, even that slight delay was probably attributable to the first messenger, young MacLachlan of Inchconnel, being decapitated by a cannonball while carrying forward with the order.

Similarly, there is an equally popular assumption built on this error that after enduring a prolonged bombardment the Jacobite attack began spontaneously in response to mounting casualties, and was led by Lady Mackintosh's men in the centre. Once again the actual sequence of events was slightly more complicated. Thanks to Lord George Murray's earlier 'changement' the Jacobite front line was now skewed in such a way that, though the right wing was standing some 500 metres from Cumberland's men, the Duke of Perth's Regiment, standing in the MacDonalds' old position on the extreme left, was still more like 700 metres away. Therefore, when a second messenger, Colonel Harry Ker of Graden, was sent forward with renewed orders to begin the attack, he very sensibly rode first to the Duke of Perth on the extreme left and then rode down the line towards Lord George Murray's position on the right, repeating the orders to each regiment as he passed. By thus starting them off in echelon he no doubt intended that the unintentional skew would be corrected and that they would all crash into the British front line at about the same time. This is why it appeared to Murray and other observers on the right that the Mackintoshes had burst forward on their own account, for unbeknown to them things were already going very badly wrong on the Jacobite left.

In the meantime, prevented by the Camerons from moving around the turf walls of the Leanach enclosure bulging out to their immediate front, the three regiments of the Atholl Brigade simply scrambled over and raced straight towards Barrell's Regiment, but the Camerons were themselves forced against the walls by an involuntary swing to the right by Lady Mackintosh's Regiment and the Frasers next to them. In part this may have been because once the men forming the rebel centre crossed the moor road where it slanted diagonally across their path, they may have moved right to avoid what certainly appeared to be boggy ground. More likely, however, that swerve also coincided with their coming within canister range of the British guns.

Until that point Captain Godwin's gunners had probably still been firing carefully at a steady rate of about one round per minute, but canister, mixed at Culloden by the heavier grapeshot, was an anti-personnel weapon intended to be fired quickly without troubling to aim and once the Highlanders came within

300 metres of the British front line the rate of fire stepped up dramatically. In the remaining 90 seconds or so required for them to close with the redcoats, Godwin's artillerymen could have fired four or even five rounds of canister or grape from each gun; each one either a tin can or canister packed with musket balls or more deadly still a canvas bag of larger cast-iron ones. At the very closest ranges it was also common to load two of them – double canister. This effectively turned each cannon into a large shotgun and, small as the little 3-pounders were, a single discharge of double canister might succeed in knocking over as many as eight to ten men. Indeed, an eyewitness named Michael Hughes wrote 'that the grapeshot made open lanes quite through them, the men dropping down by wholesale'. Little wonder then that the Highlanders should suddenly shy away from the guns at this point – and of course by so delaying the eventual confrontation give Godwin's men all the more time to fire into them. In the end it is likely that the Athollmen, Frasers and Camerons received at least 5 or 6 discharges of canister from 3 of the 5 pairs of guns, which would suggest that in the space of about two minutes they received something in the region of 200 casualties – and worse was about to come.

Whether they were trying to avoid the canister fire or the boggy ground, or both, the immediate result of this sudden swerve was that most of the Jacobite regiments in the centre and right wing became entangled together in a huge mob which rolled right down the road and impacted on Barrell's 4th Foot and Monro's 37th Foot standing on the extreme left of the British front line.

First, however, they had to brave the musketry of at least three front-line regiments: Barrell's, Monro's and Campbell's Royal Scots Fusiliers, mustering some 1,100 men in the firing line. If, as seems likely, Price's 14th Foot also got a volley in, that would increase the total number of muskets to 1,400. A corporal in Monro's afterwards related that: 'When we saw them coming towards us in great Haste and Fury, we fired at about 50 Yards Distance, which made hundreds Fall; notwithstanding which, they were so numerous, that they still advanced, and were almost upon us before we had loaden again. We immediately gave them another full fire.'

So much then for that other cherished myth of the Highlanders being able to throw themselves flat as the initial volley was fired and then leap up again to cut down the hapless soldiers as they vainly struggled to reload. Gauging the true effectiveness of eighteenth-century musket fire is far from easy. Crude statistical analyses which compare the number of rounds fired in a variety of eighteenth- and nineteenth-century battles with the number of reported casualties tend to demonstrate that only something like 1 per cent of musket balls actually hit anyone. Were that really to be the case here then the initial British volley would only have dropped about fourteen of the oncoming Jacobites, and no one would have stood around to fire a second one. The truth of the matter is that in most battles a great deal of firing was carried out at ranges much greater than the 50 yards quoted above, and was in truth pretty harmless, but at close range it was a very different matter indeed, and even allowing for a universal tendency for soldiers to fire high under stress, the percentage of hits could rise to as high as 10 per cent.

What this means in practical terms at Culloden is that the first volley of musketry may have brought down about seventy or eighty of the attacking clansmen, in addition of course to those simultaneously being killed or wounded by canister rounds. Although Price's may not have been in the right place to fire at closer range, the second and much more murderous volley will still have dropped upwards of another 100. Moreover, since all of these casualties will have been at the front of a fast-moving and fairly tightly packed mob, they themselves will have buffeted and tripped their comrades as they fell, thus increasing the confusion. The very visible effect of both canister and musketry was also vastly encouraging to the British soldiers, particularly as many of the rebels discarded their firelocks instead of firing a volley in reply. Unlike previous occasions, then, they were not intimidated by the oncoming Highlanders, and, contrary to all expectation, neither Barrell's nor Monro's 37th Foot, which was standing next to them, ran away. Instead, after firing that second volley into the rebels at point-blank range, they stood fast and charged their bayonets:

> Making a dreadful huzza, and even crying 'Run, ye dogs' they [the Jacobites] broke in between the grenadiers of Barrel and Monro; but these had given their fire according to the general direction, and then parried them with their screwed bayonets. The two cannon on that division were so well served, that when within two yards of them they received a full discharge of cartridge shot, which made a dreadful havoc; and those who crowded into the opening received a full fire from the centre of Bligh's regiment, which still increased the number of the slain.

A typical British Army bayonet of the period: 17 inches of fluted steel.

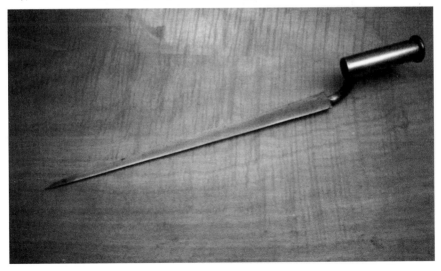

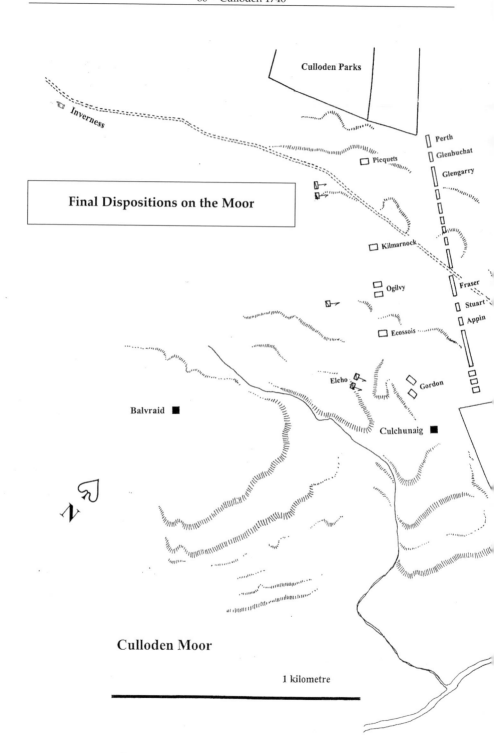

Culloden Parks

Inverness

Perth

Glenbuchat

Glengarry

Picquets

Final Dispositions on the Moor

Kilmarnock

Ogilvy

Fraser

Stuart

Appin

Ecossois

Elcho

Gordon

Balvraid

Culchunaig

Culloden Moor

1 kilometre

N

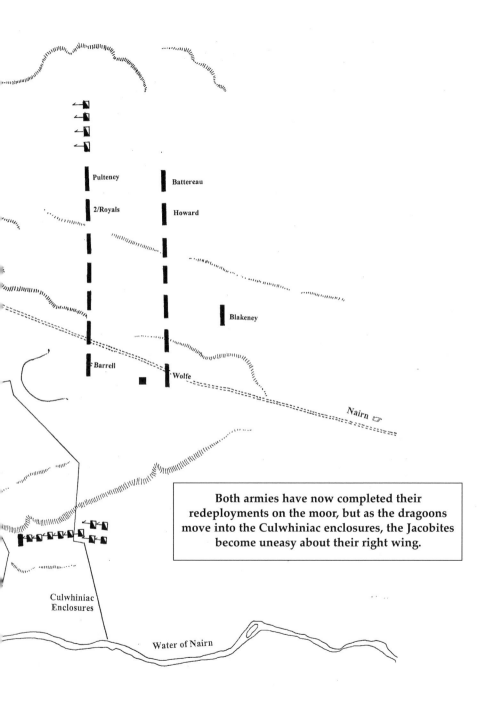

Pulteney

Battereau

2/Royals

Howard

Blakeney

Barrell

Wolfe

Nairn ☞

Culwhiniac
Enclosures

Water of Nairn

Both armies have now completed their
redeployments on the moor, but as the dragoons
move into the Culwhiniac enclosures, the Jacobites
become uneasy about their right wing.

While they were in winter quarters at Aberdeen the redcoats are said to have practised a new drill with their bayonets: 'The alteration was mightily little, but of the last consequence,' declared one British officer. 'Before this the bayonet man attacked the sword man right fronting him: now the left hand bayonet attacked the sword man fronting his next right hand man. He was then covered by the enemy's shield where open on his left, and the enemy's right open to him.' In other words, instead of thrusting at the man directly in front of him and having his bayonet parried by the clansman's targe, the soldier was expected to stick his bayonet into the unprotected armpit of the Highlander attacking the man on his immediate right, while trusting the man standing on his left to do the same for him. Although the officer then went on to say that 'This manner made an essential difference, staggered the enemy, who were not prepared to alter their way of fighting, and destroyed them in a manner rather to be conceived than told,' it is most unlikely to have worked as smoothly as that in the chaos of battle. What it no doubt did do, however, was give the men the confidence to stand their ground and employ a very different tactic which had proved itself at Falkirk three months before.

Like all good ideas it was essentially very simple. Ordinarily, the British Army employed a fire control technique called 'platoon firing' or 'platooning'. This is discussed in greater detail in Chapter 7, but essentially the firing line was broken down into a number of blocks or platoons, which then fired in a pre-arranged sequence so ordered that by the time the last platoons had fired, the first ones had reloaded and were ready to renew the cycle. By this means a steady rolling fire could be maintained for so long as bravery and cartridges lasted, but it had one fatal drawback when facing a Highland charge. The individual platoon volleys – fired by about thirty men apiece – simply could not kill enough of the enemy fast enough to stop them. After Prestonpans the British Army therefore opted to fire massed volleys by complete battalions. The risk then of course was that they might get their timing wrong and the whole lot might still be reloading when the surviving clansmen came close enough to use their broadswords – just as popular legend portrays. To avoid *that* awful possibility the front rank did not make any attempt to reload after the initial volley but instead immediately charged their bayonets to create a hedge of steel behind which the second and third ranks could reload in comparative security. According to one account the front rank of Barrell's Regiment actually knelt down at Falkirk in the manner later seen when forming square at battles such as Waterloo, but it is not clear whether they stood or knelt at Culloden.

It is clear, though, that the tactic worked. Cumberland himself expressed his satisfaction with the way Barrell's

A grenadier of Pulteney's 13th Foot demonstrating the movement 'Push your bayonet'.

and Monro's 'fairly beat them with their bayonets'. He declared: 'There was scarce a soldier or officer of Barrell's and that part of Monro's which engaged, who did not kill one or two men each with their bayonets and spontoons.' Nevertheless, they paid a heavy price for their success. In just a few desperate minutes Barrell's lost 17 killed and 108 wounded, including their commanding officer, Lieutenant Colonel Robert Rich, out of a total of just 373 officers and men. Unsurprisingly, Barrell's Regiment was burst apart and effectively overrun, temporarily losing one of its colours in the process. Similarly, Monro's afterwards reported 14 killed and 68 wounded, although proportionately these losses were actually heavier than Barrell's since only a part of the regiment was closely engaged. Nearly all of them were in fact concentrated on the regiment's left wing – and a grenadier officer, identified in a York newspaper as Lieutenant Loftus Cliffe, recorded that he had no fewer than 18 killed or wounded in his platoon alone, which must have accounted for at least half of them. 'The Hurry I am in going to collect the number of killed and wounded,' he wrote:

> scarce allows me time to tell you, that Yesterday we had the bloodiest Battle with the Rebels that ever was fought in the Memory of Man. The same Morning we march'd from Nairn, and met the Gentry about Noon near Culloden, the Lord President's House ... where we cannonaded each other for some Time; at last the Rebels advanc'd against the Left of our Line where was Barrel's Regiment, and the late Sir Robert Monro's, now Col. De Jean's. Barrel's behaved very well, but was obliged to give Way to their Torrent that bore down upon them; Their whole Force then fell upon the Left of ours where I had the Honour to command the Grenadier platoon; our Lads fought more like Devils than Men. In short we laid (to the best of my Judgement) about 1600 dead on the Spot, and finished the Affair without the Help of any other Regiment. You may judge of the Work, for I had 18 men killed and wounded in my Platoon.

This, nevertheless, was the critical point in the battle, but by now the rebel command structure had broken down completely, largely because the officers were all out in front and dropping fast. Lieutenant Colonel Charles Fraser of Inverallochy, the Aberdeenshire laird who led Lord Lovat's men, went down; Lieutenant Colonel Alexander McGillivray of Dunmaglas, commanding Lady Mackintosh's Regiment, was first wounded during the charge and then killed in the fighting, as was his second in command, Major Gillies McBean, while Donald Cameron of Lochiel similarly fell well short of the British front line, both ankles broken by canister shot. Right from the beginning, therefore, the three largest regiments were effectively rendered leaderless. Lord George Murray for his part, although notionally a lieutenant general, was now once again behaving, just as he had done at Falkirk, as if he was no more than a brigade commander. Even in this limited role he failed to exercise any meaningful control or tactical direction of the regiments around him. The fact that he initially went forward on horseback rather than on foot does suggest he intended to try to direct them, but instead, by his own

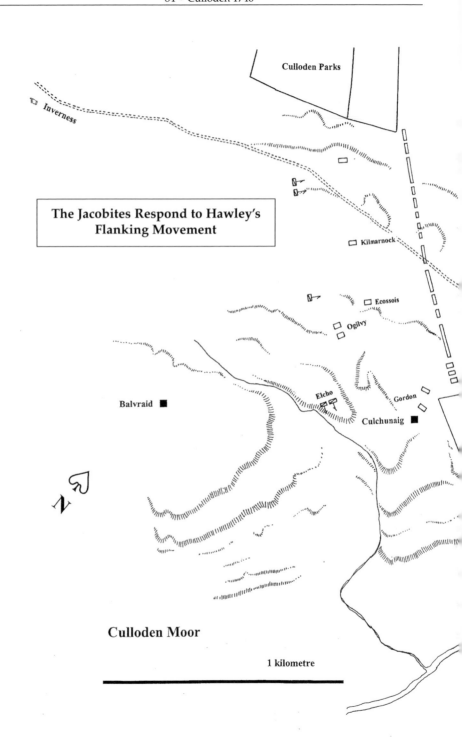

Culloden Parks

Inverness

The Jacobites Respond to Hawley's Flanking Movement

Kilmarnock

Ecossois

Ogilvy

Balvraid

Elcho

Gordon

Culchunaig

N

Culloden Moor

1 kilometre

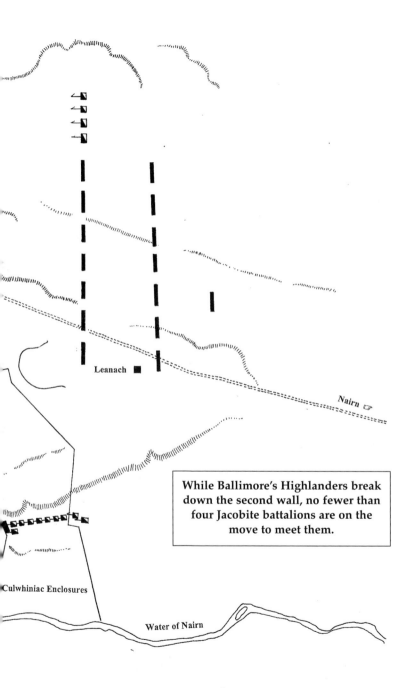

Leanach

Nairn

Culwhiniac Enclosures

Water of Nairn

While Ballimore's Highlanders break down the second wall, no fewer than four Jacobite battalions are on the move to meet them.

The death of Major Gillies McBean of Lady Mackintosh's Regiment, as splendidly depicted by Robert McIan.

account, he 'lost his horse, his periwig and bonnet ... had several cuts with broadswords in his coat, and was covered with blood and dirt'. There is no doubting then that he 'behaved ... with great gallantry', but by getting so involved in the fighting he completely lost control of his men. Had he instead kept the Athollmen back as a tactical reserve, it might then have been possible to widen the gap and exploit the breakthrough.

Instead, more and more Highlanders simply pushed up into the existing penetration instead of attacking the British units immediately to their front. Given just a little more time they might still have been able to work their way around the rapidly crumbling flank of Monro's 37th, but the doomed standby Barrell's 4th Foot had already won precious moments for Major General John Huske, commanding Cumberland's second line, to organize a counter-attack. 'The Regiment [Barrell's] behaved with uncommon resolution,' wrote James Wolfe, who also happened to be a captain in the regiment at the time: 'they were however surrounded by superiority, and would all have been destroyed had not Col. Martin with his Regiment (the left of the 2nd line of Foot) mov'd forward to their assistance, prevented mischief, and by a well timed fire destroyed a great number of them.'

Close-up of the fighting in and around Leanach as Huske's counter-attack goes in.

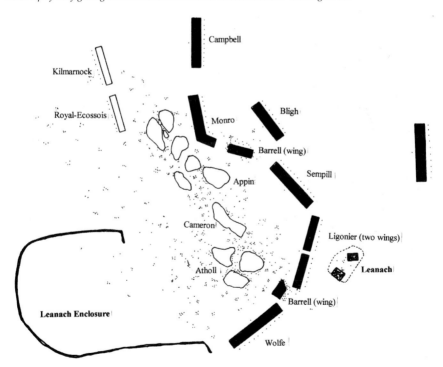

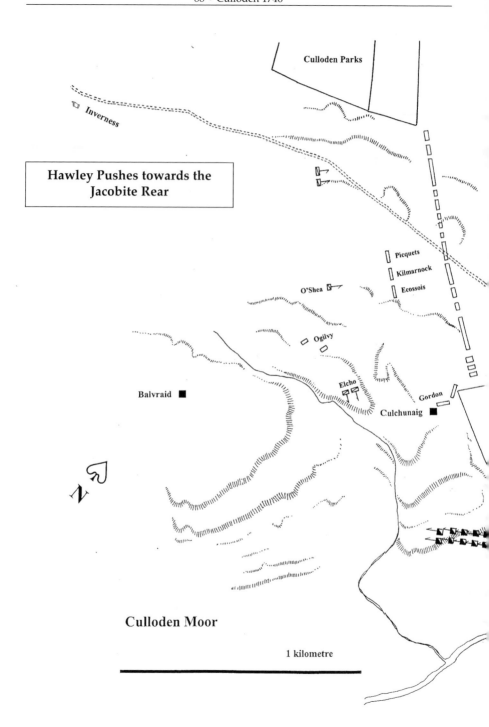

Culloden Parks

Inverness

Hawley Pushes towards the Jacobite Rear

Picquets

Kilmarnock

O'Shea

Ecossois

Ogilvy

Balvraid

Elcho

Gordon

Culchunaig

Culloden Moor

1 kilometre

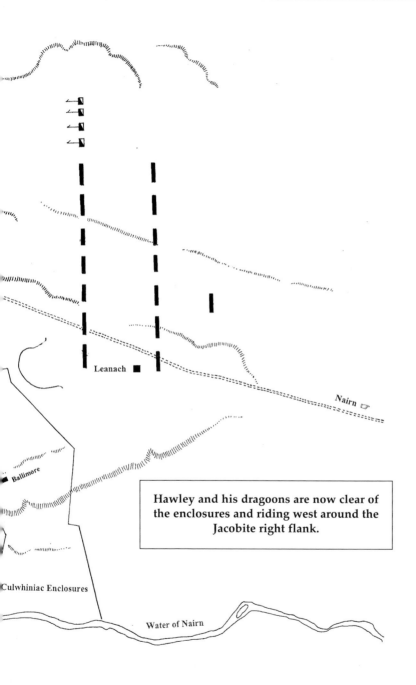

Leanach

Nairn

Ballimore

Hawley and his dragoons are now clear of
the enclosures and riding west around the
Jacobite right flank.

Culwhiniac Enclosures

Water of Nairn

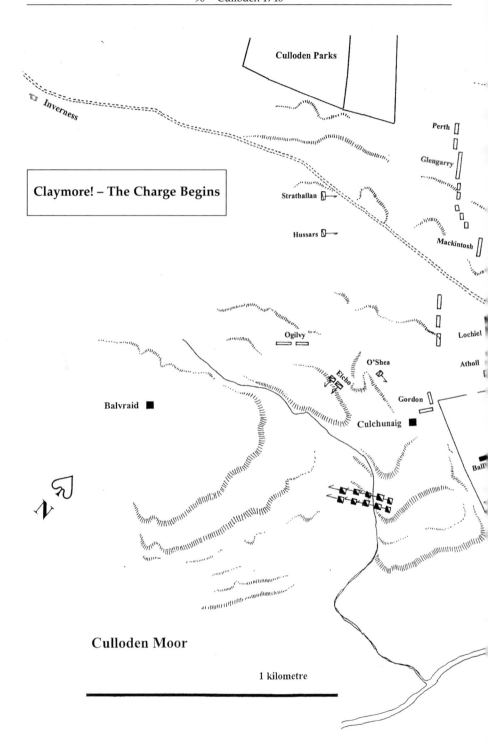

Culloden Parks

Inverness

Perth

Glengarry

Claymore! – The Charge Begins

Strathallan

Mackintosh

Hussars

Ogilvy

Lochiel

O'Shea

Atholl

Elcho

Balvraid

Gordon

Culchunaig

Ball

N

Culloden Moor

1 kilometre

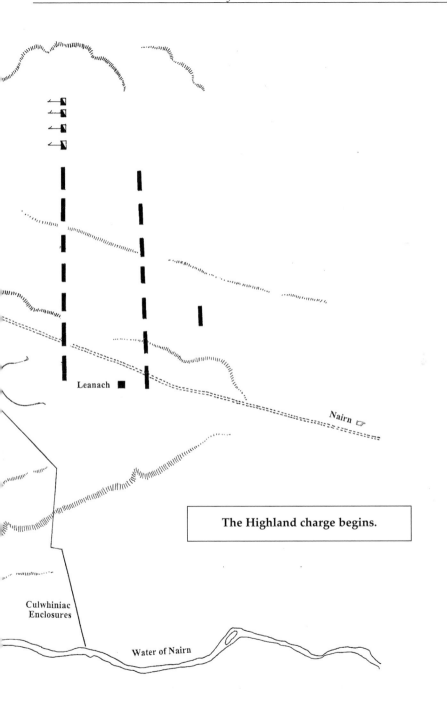

Leanach

Nairn

The Highland charge begins.

Culwhiniac
Enclosures

Water of Nairn

In fact recognizing the desperate urgency of the situation Huske had ordered forward not just Edward Wolfe's 8th Foot – who as this and other testimony makes very clear were patently not standing *en potence* to the front line at the outset – but the whole of Lord Sempill's 4th Brigade, comprising Sempill's own 25th (Edinburgh) Regiment, Harry Ligonier's 59th/48th Foot and of course Wolfe's 8th Foot, mustering a total of 1,078 bayonets, besides officers and NCOs.

In order to get into action Sempill's Brigade first had to move slightly to their left and then clear the Leanach steading, and an early sketch map by Paul Sandby shows Ligonier's 59th/48th Foot temporarily dividing into two wings in order to do so. Once past the buildings, however, according to a letter home from Captain Lieutenant James Ashe Lee of the 8th Foot, 'Poor Barrell's regiment were sorely pressed by those desperadoes and outflanked. One stand of their colours was taken; Collonel Riches hand cutt off in their defence … We marched up to the enemy, and our left, outflanking them, wheeled in upon them.' Huske had also sent forward Bligh's 20th Foot from the 2nd Brigade to plug the gap between Sempill's 25th (Edinburgh) Regiment and the hard-pressed 37th Foot. The result was that all five battalions, and perhaps some determined remnants of Barrell's 4th Foot as well, were soon formed into a large horseshoe-like arc, hemming in the rebels on three sides.

The impetus of their assault having already been blunted by the 4th and 37th Foot the Jacobite front rank was now brought to a complete halt by Huske's counter-attack. More and more men came still pushing up from the rear but were slowed by the muddy dip containing what is now known as the Well of the Dead and unable to force their way out of it were all jammed together in one huge immobile mass, flayed by a terrible crossfire at point-blank range.

Once again British accounts all relate how after their initial battalion volleys had been fired, their front-rank men stood fast with charged bayonets to protect the second and third ranks as they reloaded and fired time and again. Captain Lee of the 8th Foot reckoned 'the whole then gave them 5 or 6 fires with vast execution, while their front had nothing left to oppose us, but their pistolls and broadswords; and fire from their center and rear, (as, by this time, they were 20 or 30 deep) was vastly more fatal to themselves, than us'. This is also confirmed by the corporal of Monro's who stated that 'the Front Rank charged their Bayonets Breast high, and the Center and Rear Ranks kept a continual Firing … the Rebels designing to break or flank us; but our fire was so hot, most of us having discharged nine Shot each, that they were disappointed.' Allowing for the two volleys fired as the Highlanders charged towards them and at least one other while Sempill's brigade hurried to their assistance, that would indeed equate to five or six more at this point.

The combined strength of Sempill's brigade together with Bligh's and Monro's regiments amounted to some 1,900 men, exclusive of officers and NCOs, though enough of Barrell's men may have remained in the fight to make up about 2,000. Conservatively, therefore, and allowing for the front rank of each regiment standing fast with charged bayonets, there were at least 1,200 soldiers firing those five or six volleys. Even if only one in ten of those rounds took effect at this very short distance – firing over the front rank will have increased the tendency to shoot high – a simple calculation therefore suggests that something in the region of 700 rebels were killed or wounded in the space of just 2 or 3 terrible minutes. Hardly surprisingly, some of the survivors, including Lord George Murray, afterwards claimed that having broken through Barrell's they were fired into by a previously unsuspected battery of artillery.

By contrast the British Army's losses in this phase of the battle were negligible. Bligh's Regiment afterwards returned four men killed and sixteen wounded, while Sempill's Edinburgh Regiment had just one dead and thirteen wounded. Even then some of those casualties were probably men killed or wounded by the earlier Jacobite artillery barrage, for Wolfe's Regiment had just a single officer, the newly commissioned ensign Robert Bruce, wounded, and Ligonier's had no casualties at all.

Realizing that it was all going badly wrong, Murray tried to get the stalled assault moving again. As we have seen he lost his horse during the initial charge and then by his own testimony fought hand to hand with some of Barrell's or Monro's men, before belatedly recalling his real responsibilities. Realizing that his men would not be able to stand much longer he managed to make his way out of the press and ran back to hurry forward his own supports. To his dismay there was virtually no one left, for most of the reserves had long since been drawn off either to face the developing threat posed by Hawley's cavalry on the slope beyond Culchunaig, or to bolster the left wing.

CHAPTER VI

Blood on the Heather

Yet another of the persistent myths which cluster around this battle is the story that the three MacDonald regiments, piqued at being placed on the left wing, refused to charge at all. The story is told with a wealth of circumstantial and outwardly convincing detail, such as the claim that old Alexander McDonald of Keppoch rushed forward alone, crying that the children of his clan had forsaken him, only to be shot down by the soldiers. He certainly fell, but it is significant that at least three witnesses afterwards testified to finding his body hunched over on the ground as they came running back in retreat, and so must have advanced well beyond their fallen chief. The other MacDonald regiments also suffered heavy casualties, including young Clanranald, who was wounded in the head, and all of them must have been shot down by the muskets of Pulteney's 13th and 2/Royals for there were no cannon opposite them. This point alone is proof enough that they came forward, and indeed an Ayrshire man named Alexander Taylor, who was serving in the Royals, told how the clansmen 'came running upon our front line like troops of hungry wolves, and fought with intrepidity. But the thunder of our fire, and the continuation of it, began to slacken their fury'.

Nevertheless, the story that the MacDonalds hung back grew afterwards and was embellished upon, particularly by Lord George Murray's supporters, simply because it explained the Jacobite defeat. Had the MacDonalds charged too, so it is alleged, Murray and his men would not have been left to bear the brunt of the battle by themselves. If the MacDonalds had gone forward and repeated the success of the right wing, then Culloden might have been a Jacobite victory. In fact there was never any realistic chance of them changing the course of events. Far from refusing to charge, the MacDonalds, together with Perth's and Glenbuchat's men on their left, all started forward at pretty much the same time as the others. However, owing to the way in which the Jacobite front line was skewed in relation to the British one, they had something like 200 metres further to go than Murray's men on the right, and moreover they also had to cross much boggier ground from the very outset. In fact Captain James Johnstone, who fought at Culloden as a volunteer in Glengarry's Regiment, afterwards complained that it was not merely boggy but 'covered with water which reached halfway up the leg'. He of course had good reason to emphasize the difficulties which he and his comrades faced, but the state of the ground on this part of the field is confirmed by various British Army sources, similarly complaining of mud and water coming up to their knees – and by Cumberland's initial reluctance to post any of his cavalry on this wing.

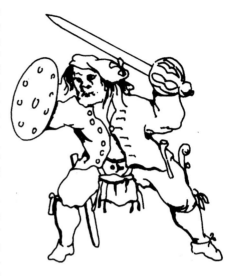

Alexander McDonald of Keppoch, who was killed at Culloden.

In all these circumstances it is hardly surprising that the rebels' advance on the left wing was so very much slower and ultimately more reluctant, or that, finding the regulars unintimidated by their laborious progress, they should have aborted the assault without making contact. 'They came running on in their wild manner,' declared Cumberland himself, 'and upon the Right where I had placed Myself, imagining the greatest Push would be there, they came down three several Times within a Hundred Yards of our Men, firing their pistols and brandishing their Swords, but the Royals and Pulteneys hardly took their Firelocks from their shoulders.' The fact of the matter was that the Highlanders were frustrated by the regulars' failure to obligingly run away. 'Our left flinches,' wrote Sullivan. 'The Duke of Perth runs to Clanronald's Regiment takes their Collors & tells them from that day forth he'l call himself MacDonel if they gain the day. Lord John [Drummond] & Sullivan brings up the left again.' This time Johnstone thought they got within 20 paces of Cumberland's line and certainly close enough for him to consider it worth discharging his blunderbuss at the redcoats. He even thought that if the Jacobite right wing could have stayed in the fight a few moments longer, he and his MacDonald comrades could still have won the day. It was of course no more than wishful thinking, and all the time the casualties were mounting.

The little units on the MacDonalds' right were faring particularly badly, perhaps because they had become relatively isolated in the centre of the increasingly ragged Jacobite front line. The Chisholms, the combined battalion of MacLeans and MacLachlans, and Farquharson of Monaltrie's men all pretty well disintegrated. In fact all the officers in the little independent company formed by the Chisholms of Strathglas were killed or wounded, while Colonel Lachlan MacLachlan was fatally wounded by a cannon shot – an eyewitness gruesomely described how his 'guts were laid over his horse's neck' – while no fewer than thirteen of Monaltrie's officers fell. Both the Chisholms and Monaltrie's men also lost their colours, and in

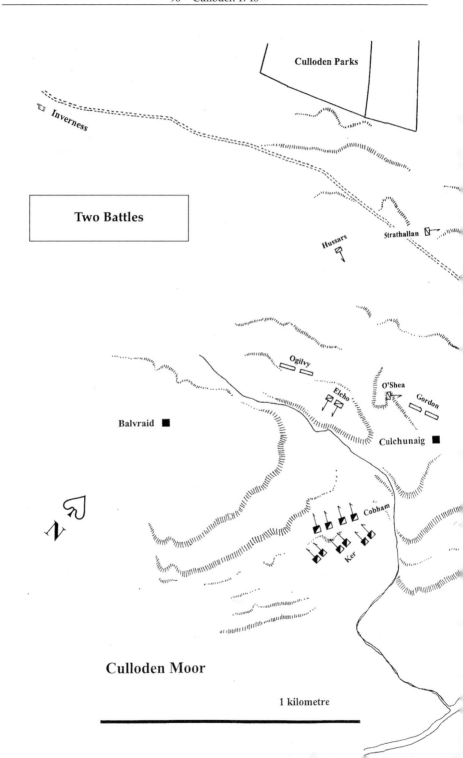

Culloden Parks

Inverness

Two Battles

Hussars

Strathallan

Ogilvy

O'Shea

Elcho

Gordon

Balvraid

Culchunaig

Cobham

Ker

N

Culloden Moor

1 kilometre

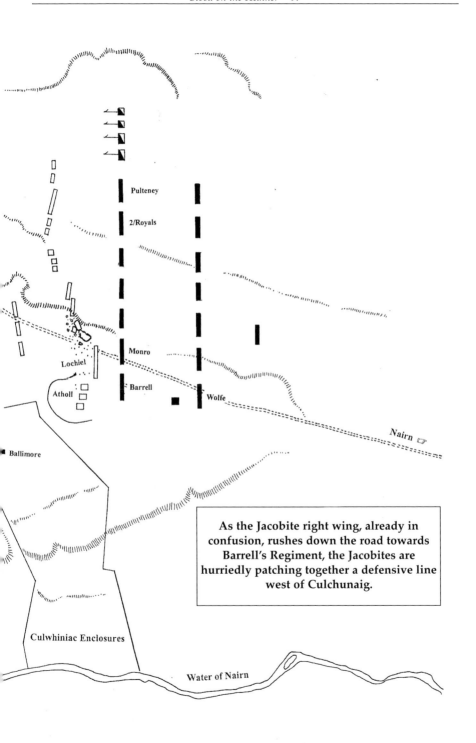

Pulteney

2/Royals

Monro

Lochiel

Atholl

Barrell

Wolfe

Ballimore

Nairn

As the Jacobite right wing, already in
confusion, rushes down the road towards
Barrell's Regiment, the Jacobites are
hurriedly patching together a defensive line
west of Culchunaig.

Culwhiniac Enclosures

Water of Nairn

the circumstances MacLachlan's may well be one of the unidentified ones. Out on the extreme left flank Perth's and Glenbuchat's regiments seem to have advanced with the MacDonalds, but got on the receiving end of at least one volley from Pulteney's and soon retired, leaving Major Robert Stewart pinned beneath his dead horse. As their leaders were shot down one after the other the MacDonalds too began to give way. Sensing his advantage Cumberland himself then galloped across to the two little troops of Cobham's 10th Dragoons (numbering about ninety officers and men in total) and, according to one, 'clapping some of them on the shoulders, call'd out "One Brush, my Lads, for the Honour of old Cobham"; upon which, rather like Devils than Men they broke through the Enemy's Flank and a total Rout followed'.

It was not quite so dramatic as that, of course, for the dragoons had first to carefully splash their way across the very same boggy ground which had slowed the Jacobite advance and which James Johnstone earlier thought 'well chosen to protect us from the cavalry of the enemy'. As a result, Perth's and Glenbuchat's regiments had certainly disengaged and were well away before the attack came in, and it is also possible that the MacDonalds were also falling back towards the Inverness road before the Dragoons got clear of the bog.

To cover their retreat Sullivan appears to have brought up the Irish Picquets, who had been one of just three battalions left in reserve at that point, and consequently when Murray came running back in search of support for the collapsing right wing, he found just two battalions still unengaged: the blue-bonneted Royal Ecossois and Lord Kilmarnock's newly raised Footguards. Both regiments followed him forward, but it was already too late. 'I brought up two regiments from our second line, after this, who gave their fire,' said Murray, 'but nothing could be done – all was lost.' And so it was. As the surviving clansmen dissolved into rout Kilmarnock's men fired a hasty volley and then ran back with them, and although the Royal Ecossois fell back too, they at least tried to do so with a little more dignity, as befitted their status as regulars. After exchanging token volleys with Campbell's 21st (Royal Scots Fusiliers) they then began to fall back in good order. Sensibly enough they first moved to their right and then retired along the outside of the Culwhiniac enclosure wall, where they were masked from artillery fire by the Leanach enclosure. With luck they might have got clean away. Unfortunately, they had reckoned without the half-battalion of loyalist Highlanders commanded by Captain Colin Campbell of Ballimore.

As we have seen, Ballimore and his men had cleared the way for Hawley's dragoons by breaking down the Culwhiniac enclosure walls. However, once all the dragoons were through the enclosures and out onto the open slopes below Culchunaig, Hawley decided to leave the Highlanders behind. It is possible that he may have instructed them to engage Lord Lewis Gordon's men who had been lining the wall up by Culchunaig at that time, and certainly Captain Duncan Campbell of the Argyle Militia unequivocally wrote that 'we were ordered to attack them'. Nevertheless, on balance Hawley probably thought that now they had done their job it would be best to leave them behind in order to avoid any unfortunate mistakes or uncertainty. From now on, any man in tartan clothes would be assumed to be hostile. Nevertheless, since Hawley neglected specifically to order Ballimore to retire to the baggage train and may or may not have indicated that any rebels inside the enclosure were fair game, the gallant captain very properly decided to get in on the fight after all.

Moving up the slope inside the park Ballimore appears to have initially opened fire at long range on some of the Jacobites – perhaps Lord Ogilvy's men, lining the re-entrant near Culchunaig. This firing was of little more than nuisance value at first, but 'though few were killed by reason of the distance yet many were wounded, especially in the legs and thighs'. All the same this was petty stuff, but then along came a much more worthwhile target. Campbell of Airds gleefully reported that: 'Ballimore & his command were ordered to break down them Dykes & make way for the Horse which they Executed, & taking advantage of the Second Dyke as a Breast Work fire Closs on a strong party of the Rebels that then formed the Right, Composed of Lord John Drummond's men being part of the Enemy's second line.' A high concentration of bullets discovered during recent archaeological investigations clearly pinpoints the site of this ambush as being in the otherwise sheltered corner where the Leanach and Culwhiniac enclosures met. Just how much damage Ballimore's volley inflicted on the Royal Ecossois is unknown, but the regulars fired a withering volley in reply. Campbell of Airds sadly reported afterwards that 'It was in passing a slap [opening] in the second Dyke that Ballimore was Shot Dead, and that Achnaba received his wound of which he Dyed next day.' Six other men in Ballimore's own company of the 64th Highlanders were afterwards returned as dead, and three were wounded in this brief firefight. When their graves were rediscovered in the following century it was noted that, though Ballimore was killed standing in the open gateway, most of his dead had apparently been shot through the head, clearly indicating that they themselves were firing from behind the wall at the time.

Short and sharp though this vicious little exchange proved to be, it was still sufficient to drive Kilmarnock's men and the Royal Ecossois back out onto the open moor and, unwittingly, throw them into the path of Hawley's dragoons.

Up until this point General Hawley, rather to the frustration of some of his junior officers (including young James Wolfe), had been content to remain passively observing the strong force of Jacobites posted along the crest in front of him. This, as we have seen, comprised the two battalions of Lord Ogilvy's Forfarshire Regiment, and two others raised by Lord Lewis Gordon; John Gordon of Avochie's Strathbogie battalion and James Moir of Stonywood's Aberdeen battalion; and Lord Elcho's Lifeguards and the greater part of Fitzjames's Cavalerie. Of themselves they presented a significant barrier, especially as they were on the other side of what amounted to a fairly substantial ditch. Indeed, one of Lord Elcho's officers, Major James Maxwell of Kirconnell, remembered that 'Lord George [Murray] ordered the Guards and Fitzjames's horse quite to the right flank, and made them form opposite to the dragoons on the brink of a hollow way; the ascent was somewhat steep on both sides, so that neither could pass safely in the presence of the other.' Moreover, since the Jacobites were above the dragoons, there was of course no way of telling whether they had anything else in reserve. Had Hawley

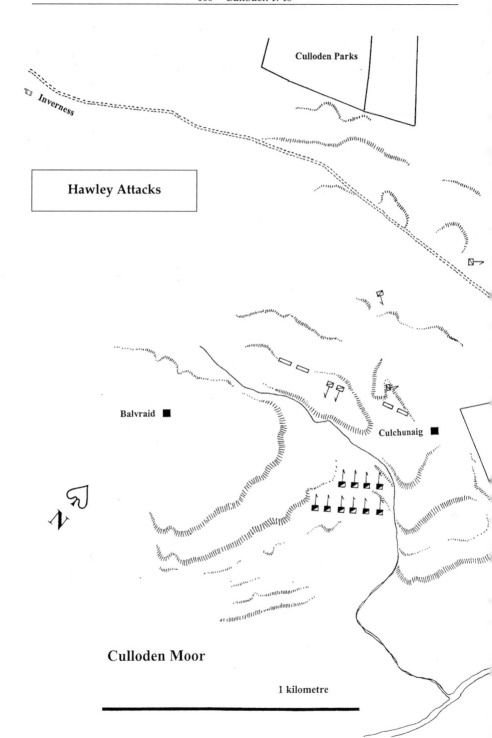

Culloden Parks

Inverness

Hawley Attacks

Balvraid ■

Culchunaig ■

Culloden Moor

1 kilometre

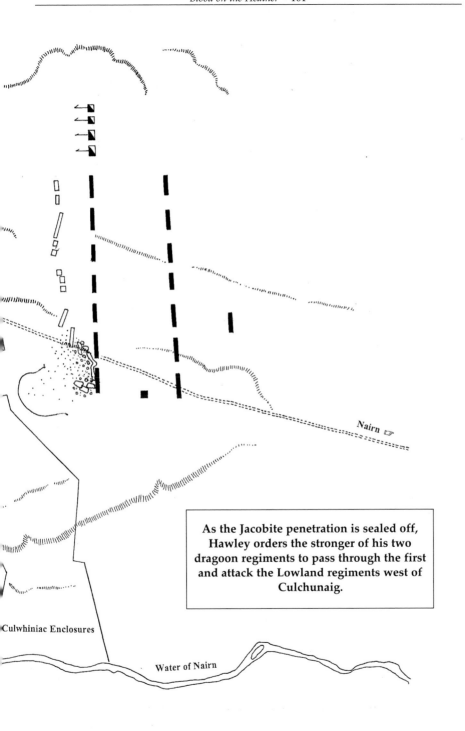

Nairn

As the Jacobite penetration is sealed off, Hawley orders the stronger of his two dragoon regiments to pass through the first and attack the Lowland regiments west of Culchunaig.

Culwhiniac Enclosures

Water of Nairn

been more aggressive the battle could easily have been even more of a disaster for the Jacobites, and after revisiting the field five years later, James Wolfe grumbled to his father that 'The actors [Hawley and Bland] shine in the world too high and bright to be eclipsed; but it is plain they don't borrow much of their glory from their performance on that occasion.' Nevertheless, in the circumstances this early caution was understandable, but now, however, as Wolfe related, 'as soon as the Rebels began to give way and the Fire of the Foot slacken'd, he (Hawley) ordered Genl Bland to charge the rest of them with three squadrons, and Cobham to support him with two'.

So far, Cobham's, as the senior regiment of the two, had led the advance, but one of its squadrons was of course over on Cumberland's left wing, which meant it was only 180 strong, and so Hawley decided to employ the 300 strong Ker's 11th Dragoons to break through the defensive line on the ridge above. Accordingly, Bland took the six troops through the intervals in Cobham's four, across the re-entrant and on up the slope. The rebels were evidently already beginning to withdraw by this time, but nevertheless unleashed a surprisingly

A contemporary illustration of a French cavalryman, providing a useful picture of the likely appearance of the red-coated Fitzjames's Cavalerie.

The altogether scruffier-looking Bagot's Hussars after sketches by the Penicuik artist. Other contemporary eyewitnesses recorded they had reddish fur caps and wore close-fitting tartan jackets or waistcoats.

effective volley. Ker's had three men killed and three others wounded at Culloden, which at first sight appears negligible, but the regiment also reported the loss of no fewer than nineteen horses, so the fight may not have been quite such a walkover after all. This partial check may explain why these particular rebels subsequently got away without further molestation, leading Wolfe to complain to his father that 'You would not have left those ruffians the only possible means of conquest, nor suffer multitudes to go off unhurt with the power to destroy.'

Once Ker's had cleared the way, Cobham's had a much easier time of it and, emerging straight onto the moor, gave some of the rebels a very nasty surprise indeed. Not realizing that the British cavalry were already roaming about in the Jacobite rear area, Lord Kilmarnock, whose regiment seems to have disintegrated, blithely rode up to Cobham's Dragoons, mistaking them for the red-coated Fitzjames's Cavalerie. He was lucky not to be summarily shot there and then, although he would later be given a fair trial and executed some months later. The Royal Ecossois, having disengaged from Ballimore's men, fared little better, for at about this time, as he recalled, an English volunteer named John Daniel met Lord John Drummond, who 'desired I would come off with him, telling me all was over and shewing me his regiment just by him, surrounded'. In actual fact the Royal Ecossois may have been retiring by alternate wings, or battalions. While part of the regiment, under Lieutenant Colonel Lord Lewis Drummond, certainly surrendered on the field after losing about fifty killed or wounded, their distinctive colours, bearing a large thistle superimposed on the cross of St Andrew, were not captured with them. On the contrary both the colours and a substantial number of men led by Major Matthew Hale succeeded in getting away with the rest of the low-country regiments which had stood above the re-entrant.

At any event this particular fight may also have given the Prince himself precious time to escape. When the artillery bombardment began, many of Godwin's cannonballs were pitched too high and flew over the heads of the men in the front line to cause a certain amount of confusion and dismay in the Jacobite rear. Oddly enough, both the cavalry officers on the Jacobite left, Lord Strathallan and Major Bagot, were badly wounded, presumably by cannon shot, and there is anecdotal evidence that in the centre Balmerino's troop of Lifeguards were particularly badly hit, while even Prince Charles had his horse injured by these random shots and a groom, named Thomas Ca, standing nearby was decapitated. 'The Prince, observing this disagreeable position, and without answering any end whatever,' wrote Robert Strange, one of the Lifeguards:

> ordered us down to a covered way, which was a little towards our right, and where we were less annoyed by the Duke's cannon; he himself with his aides-de-camp, rode along the line towards the right, animating the soldiers. The guards had scarce been a minute or two in this position, when the small arms began from the Duke's army, and kept up a constant fire; that instant, as it were, one of the aides-de-camp returned, and desired us to join the Prince.

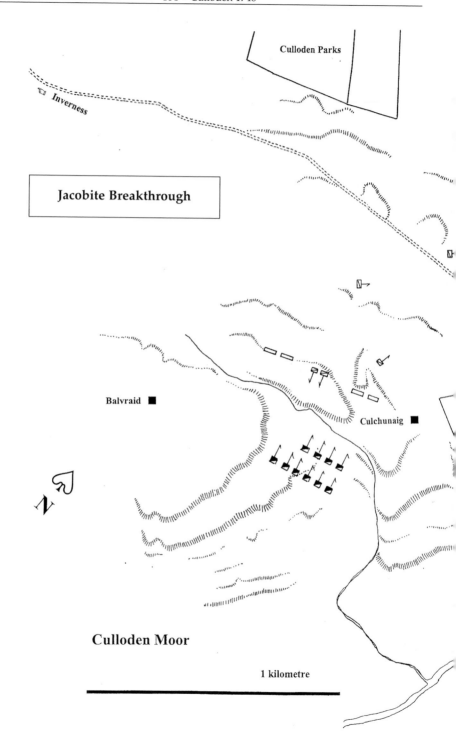

Culloden Parks

Inverness

Jacobite Breakthrough

Balvraid

Culchunaig

N

Culloden Moor

1 kilometre

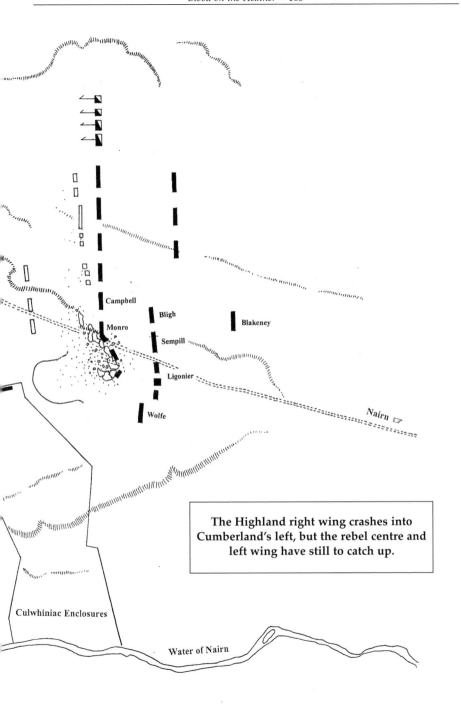

Campbell

Bligh

Blakeney

Monro

Sempill

Ligonier

Wolfe

Nairn ☞

The Highland right wing crashes into
Cumberland's left, but the rebel centre and
left wing have still to catch up.

Culwhiniac Enclosures

Water of Nairn

When the MacDonalds finally broke the Prince appears to have been rallying Perth's and Glenbuchat's regiments, but, seeing Lord George Murray's right wing collapse as well, Sullivan immediately rode to Captain O'Shea at the head of the Prince's escort squadron and shouted: 'yu see all is going to pot. Yu can be of no great succor, so before a general deroute wch will soon be, Seize upon the Prince & take him off.'

At first the Prince stubbornly refused to retire, 'notwithstanding all that can be told him,' but then Sullivan spotted Cobham's Dragoons and Kingston's Horse moving forward, and:

> seeing this Regiment marching towards our left, as if they were to cut our retrait runs to the Prince, and tells him that he has no time to lose that he'l be surrounded immediately if he does not retir. 'Well,' says the Prince, 'they wont take me alive.' Sullivan prays him to look behind him, & that he'd see the whole moor cover'd with men that were going off & that half the Army was away.

This time, O'Shea did his duty and hustled him away safely, accompanied by Perth's and Glenbuchat's men.

The Prince's retreat, probably unwittingly, was covered both by the Royal Ecossois and by the Irish Picquets, although exactly what happened to the latter is a touch obscure. Sullivan simply says that '[Brigadier Walter] Stapleton makes an evolution or two, fires at the Dragoons & obliges them to retire ... the Picquets throws themselves into the Park yt was on our left, continues there fire.' With them too was a French engineer officer named Du Saussey who had brought up another gun, probably one of the light 'Swedish' 4-pounders, and there they remained in the north-eastern corner of the Culloden Parks for some time, making a thorough nuisance of themselves until Belford and Godwin brought up a number of Coehorn mortars to silence Du Saussey's gun, and with Stapleton mortally wounded the gallant little band at last surrendered.

By that time they were probably the last formed Jacobite unit still on the field. As it broke up the rebel army effectively divided itself in two. The four Lowland battalions which had been posted above the re-entrant, together with a part of the Royal Ecossois, retained some kind of order and retired southwards, crossed the Water of Nairn and eventually made their way to Ruthven Barracks. However, with this particular escape-route cut almost at once by the dragoons moving up from the south, most of the Highland regiments from the front line were forced to take the understandable but fatal course of running straight back down the road to Inverness. It was just the situation which every cavalryman dreams of. Led by Bland, all of the dragoons set off after the fugitives and 'gave Quarter to None but about Fifty French Officers and Soldiers He picked up in his Pursuit'.

Although the vigorous and undoubtedly bloody pursuit was afterwards represented in some quarters as tantamount to a war crime, it was in reality nothing out of the ordinary, and indeed the Highlanders themselves had proved themselves equally ruthless when the position was reversed. As James Wolfe, who almost certainly took part in the pursuit himself, remarked, 'The Rebels, besides their natural inclinations, had orders not to give quarter to our men. We had an opportunity of avenging ourselves for that and many other things, and indeed we did not neglect it, as few Highlanders were made prisoners as possible.'

As the first of those fugitives came running down the Inverness road they were met by a battalion of Frasers commanded by their chief's son, Simon Fraser, the Master of Lovat. Popular legend has it that, realizing all was lost, the Master promptly faced his men about and marched them straight back to Inverness with their colours still flying and pipes playing. While there is absolutely no reason to doubt the story, what happened next is far more intriguing. Having safely returned to Inverness, the Frasers then needed to cross the bridge over the River Ness to reach their own country, and there are two different but not inconsistent stories regarding this bridge. One, quite plausibly, has the Master of Lovat proposing to defend it until he was dissuaded by some of the burgesses, who quite understandably wanted to distance the town from the rebels. The other story, much more improbably, has the bridge seized by a party of the Argyle Militia who somehow preceded the dragoons into the town and vainly tried to block the Jacobite retreat. At first sight this particular story seems nonsensical, yet James Johnstone recalled hearing a short but intense burst of firing as he fled past the town, which does point to some kind of a fight. Yet if it was not the Argyles, then the most sensible explanation is to combine the two stories and conclude that the rather slippery Master of Lovat changed sides, and that his men tried to block the bridge against their erstwhile colleagues. This might also in turn explain why the Master was afterwards treated so leniently by the government, and why he eventually died as a lieutenant general in the British Army.

'We had the bloodiest Battle with the Rebels that ever was fought in the Memory of Man,' wrote Lieutenant Cliffe, yet his own and Barrell's Regiment aside, the British Army's casualties were on the whole comparatively light. Regimental returns recorded just 50 dead and 259 wounded, although a high proportion of the latter must have died soon afterwards. Lieutenant Dally of Monro's, for example, was officially returned as wounded in Cumberland's dispatch, but had already died by the following day when Lieutenant Cliffe penned his celebrated letter. Similarly, only 19 out of the 68 rank and file returned by the regiment as wounded afterwards survived to claim pensions from Chelsea, while just 29 survived out of the 104 rank and file returned as wounded in Barrell's 4th Foot. In short, nearly 200 of the wounded appear to have subsequently died, some of them in Inverness but enough of them in the makeshift field hospitals on the moor to explain why the burial trench recently surveyed in the 'Field of the English' is much bigger than required for the initial count of 50 dead.

It was impossible of course to compile accurate returns of rebel casualties, but most estimates reckoned that around 1,500 Jacobites were killed or wounded, besides an initial total of 326 prisoners reported in Cumberland's dispatch. However, on closer examination it turns out that this figure included 172 of the Earl of Cromartie's men taken prisoner by loyalists in a neat little action at Dunrobin on the day before. The true figures for prisoners actually taken on the day are

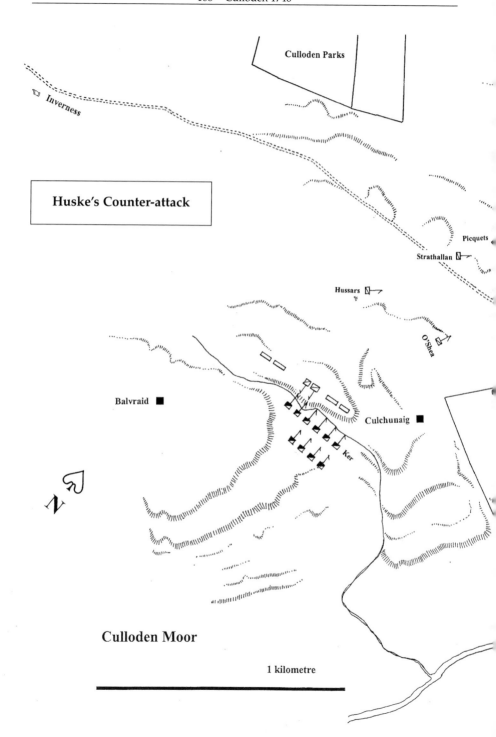

Culloden Parks

Inverness

Huske's Counter-attack

Picquets

Strathallan

Hussars

O'Shea

Balvraid

Culchunaig

Ker

N

Culloden Moor

1 kilometre

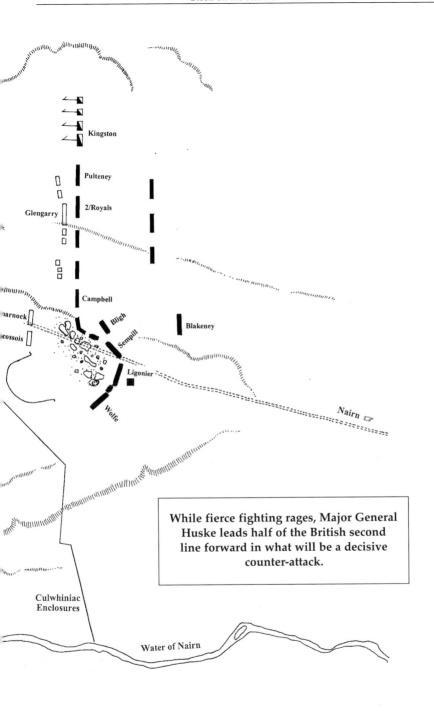

While fierce fighting rages, Major General Huske leads half of the British second line forward in what will be a decisive counter-attack.

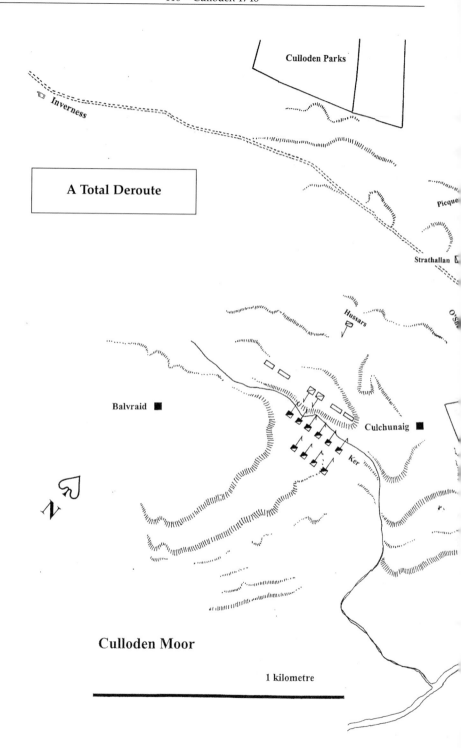

Culloden Parks

Inverness

A Total Deroute

Picque

Strathallan

Hussars

Balvraid

Culchunaig

Ker

N

Culloden Moor

1 kilometre

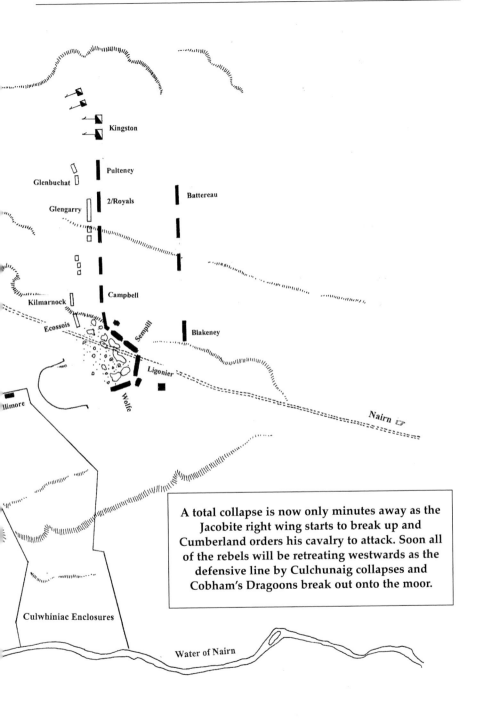

Kingston

Pulteney
Glenbuchat
2/Royals
Glengarry
Battereau

Campbell
Kilmarnock
Ecossois
Blakeney
Sempill
Ligonier
Wolfe
llimore
Nairn

A total collapse is now only minutes away as the Jacobite right wing starts to break up and Cumberland orders his cavalry to attack. Soon all of the rebels will be retreating westwards as the defensive line by Culchunaig collapses and Cobham's Dragoons break out onto the moor.

Culwhiniac Enclosures

Water of Nairn

154 rebels and 222 'French' officers and soldiers. Afterwards allegations were rife that hundreds of rebel wounded were executed out of hand, although the British Army's attitude was summed up by Lieutenant Cliffe of the 37th Foot, who wrote that:

> Our Regiment had ample revenge for the Loss of our late Colonel, Sir Robert [Monro], and the rest of our Officers, whom the Scoundrels murdered in cold blood, but (as I told Lord Kilmarnock) we had ample Revenge in hors. For I can with great Truth assure you, not one that attack'd us escaped alive, for we gave no Quarters nor would accept of any.

Nevertheless, Cliffe was very obviously talking about what happened in the heat of the battle itself, and the total number of prisoners held at Inverness rose dramatically over the next few days as a surprising number of wounded rebels were brought in from the moor. While it was freely admitted that a number of them were instead executed out of hand, these were on the whole isolated incidents carried out by unsupervised parties of the despised 'Vestry men' – conscripts rounded up by parish constables – who had been assigned to the battlefield clearance and prisoner-handling duties which the regulars avoided.

Having taken possession of the town, released the British prisoners held there and replaced them with Jacobite ones, the Duke of Cumberland paused to take stock. The war in Flanders was now his main priority and he was understandably reluctant to take his army into the hills in pursuit of the rebels. At first the indications were that he might not have to. After the battle upwards of 1,500 men assembled at Ruthven Barracks, but then orders came from the Prince, directing them to 'shift for themselves'. Similar orders must have been sent to other units gathering at Fort Augustus, and for all practical purposes the Jacobite Army was disbanded on 18 April. Those officers and men of the Royal Ecossois and Fitzjames's Horse who were confident of being treated as prisoners of war returned to Inverness and surrendered there on 19 April, but everyone else simply made for home, or else tried to escape abroad. Cumberland therefore made an offer of amnesty to the rebel leaders as well as to their followers, but on 30 April two French frigates, the *Mars* and the *Bellona*, arrived in Loch nan Uamh and landed a quantity of supplies, including some £35,000 in gold. Without it Cameron of Lochiel and the other surviving clan chiefs might have responded positively to Cumberland's amnesty, but instead they took the fatal decision to fight on. On 8 May, at a meeting held at Muirlaggan, near the head of Loch Arkaig, Lochiel, Lochgarry, Clanranald and MacDonald of Barisdale all agreed to call out their men once more and bring them to a rendezvous at Invermallie on 18 May, where they would be joined by the remains of Keppoch's men, and Cluny MacPherson's regiment, which had not been at Culloden.

Instead, the rendezvous turned into a complete fiasco which belies the arguments of armchair strategists that the Jacobites could have conducted a successful guerrilla campaign in the hills. Clanranald never appeared, while Lochgarry and Barisdale brought in just 300 men and promptly dispersed again in search of food. Only Lochiel was left at Achnacarry, with the 300 men remaining of his once strong regiment. He still entertained some hopes of joining with Cluny, but unbeknown to him the MacPhersons had surrendered to the Earl of Loudoun the day before.

Worse still, Cumberland, his patience exhausted, had moved into the hills. His reluctance is evident from the fact that he waited a whole month at Inverness, but having taken the decision to move he acted quickly and decisively. Fort Augustus was reoccupied on 17 May by three regular battalions and eight Highland companies. Incredibly, Lochiel was unaware of this until next morning, when he learned that a body of Highlanders was approaching and jumped to the hopeful conclusion that they were Barisdale's men returning: 'but he was soon undeceived by some out-scouts he had placed at proper distances who told him these men were certainly Loudoun's, for they saw the red crosses in their bonnets'. Recognizing that it was all over at last, Lochiel ordered his men to disperse without fighting, but by then it was too late to avert the punitive expeditions which began a week later and continued throughout the summer. Aimed at destroying the clans' ability to sustain a partisan war which they had already abandoned, the campaign was necessarily cruel, but, though in time popular historians would weave it into a legacy of bitterness, it would prove no hindrance to the recruitment of Highland regiments for the British Army, including one raised by Simon Fraser, the sometime Master of Lovat, who would fight under James Wolfe at the taking of Quebec.

Culloden marked the end for the Stuart dynasty, of course, but the battle was really fought to determine whether Scotland would reassert her recently surrendered independence or commit herself fully to the union with England and the promise of empire – and that outcome was never seriously in doubt.

CHAPTER VII

The Armies

To a very large extent, the popular view of the British Army at Culloden is still coloured by contemporary propaganda and it is all too often referred to as the Hanoverian Army. Yet in reality it was nothing of the sort, for King George's Hanoverian soldiers were in Germany, where they belonged. Those who fought at Culloden on the other hand were indeed British soldiers. In fact, four out of Cumberland's sixteen infantry battalions at Culloden were Scottish regiments, and there were plenty other Scottish officers and soldiers standing in the ranks of what were notionally English regiments. It is slightly ironic, for example, that the only casualty returned by Wolfe's 8th Foot was Ensign Robert Bruce from Edinburgh. What is more, as some remarkable eyewitness sketches by an artist from Penicuik reveal, they were also very ordinary British soldiers who, apart from the colour of their shabby red coats, would probably not have looked out of place in the Falklands 250 years later – and this is an impression which is amply confirmed by surviving diaries, letters and official records.

Notwithstanding some fairly obvious differences, the two armies which faced each other at Culloden were in fact fundamentally similar in their social origins, organisation and equipment. It is easy to get the impression that the Jacobite army was little more than a tumultuous mob of ferociously armed Highland warriors, but the rebel army strove hard to be a proper one with organised regiments of infantry and cavalry, a train of artillery, a general staff and all the other supporting services.

In contrasting the two, the British Army had of course an edge in that it was an existing institution honed by years of service, while the rebel one did not exist in any form before late August of 1745.

Most regular soldiers were infantrymen, belonging to regiments which at this time were normally identified by the name of their nominal commanding officer, or less commonly by a number denoting their seniority in the Army List; thus Barrell's 4th Foot and Sempill's 25th Foot. With the exception of the 1st Royals [or Royal Scots], each regiment comprised a single battalion which in turn was made up of ten companies, one of which was designated as the grenadier company. Originally

Despite their scruffy appearance these men sketched by the Penicuik artist are in fact British regulars, easily identified by their knapsacks, canteens and swords. Note how their tricorne hats have become rather more practical slouched ones.

assault troops, grenadiers were no longer required to throw grenades and nor were they, as popular legend would have it, the tallest and strongest men in the battalion, but rather the older, steadier men who could be relied upon in a crisis. Indeed, when a battalion was deployed for action, the grenadiers were split into two platoons and positioned to guard the right and left flanks of the firing line. In theory companies should have mustered 60 men and 3 officers apiece, but this was rarely the case on active service and as we saw earlier Cumberland's regiments can only have had between 30 and 40 men to a company.

Jacobite regiments aspired to a similar organisation, although in practice they fell even further from the ideal. Unsurprisingly in the circumstances, commissions to raise regiments and companies were issued rather optimistically. While a number of clan chiefs such as Cameron of Locheil were capable of levying large regiments, others, such as the Laird of MacLachlan, could rather more typically muster only a handful of followers. Similarly some Lowland gentlemen such as Lord Ogilvy and the Duke of Perth, were able to raise respectable sized units, while others were much less successful. Thus, in Aberdeenshire, James Crichton of Auchengoul obtained a colonel's commission but seems to have recruited never more than about thirty men, and probably a good deal fewer. The inevitable result was that in the early days these small regiments with far too many officers led to all sorts of organisational problems and Colonel Sullivan grumbled that "all was confused... such a chiefe of a tribe had sixty men, another thirty, another twenty, more or lesse; they would not mix or seperat, & wou'd have double officers, yt is two Captns & two Lts, to each Compagny, strong or weak... but by little & little, were brought into a certain regulation."

This was confirmed in a letter written by Alexander Grant, younger of Shewglie, to his father shortly after Prestonpans expressing pleasure that he and his followers had been assigned to Glengarry's Regiment rather than Locheil's, for "the small numbers we had when we came here would never have brought Patrick and I to the station we are in, besides Locheil has too many of his own friends to make interest for, his gentlemen are so numerous that he is obliged to have double officers and I'm convinced that our Colonel will make as much interest for us as for any of his own friends."

Other examples included Crichton of Auchengoul, who was drafted with his men into a regiment being raised for Lord Kilmarnock, and the Macleans and Maclachlans who were rolled together into a single regiment.

On both sides recruitment was supposedly a voluntary process. In the 1740s most of those who joined the British Army were still young and footloose agricultural labourers and handloom weavers, rather than the urban slum-dwellers spawned by the agricultural and industrial revolutions later in the century Other occupations were represented too, but between the two of them the countrymen picked up at provincial hiring fairs and markets, and the weavers accounted for most of King George's recruits. A soldier's life could indeed be hard at times, but there was no denying its compensations: drill might be strenuous, but less so than labouring in the fields; soldiers were regularly clothed and properly fed and if their pay was low it was at least constant – unlike in civilian life. Moreover, when not actually on active service soldiers were normally allowed to supplement the King's pay by taking on casual work in their surprisingly abundant spare time. All of them were in theory enlisted for life, but in practice this normally meant being discharged in their forties. However, at least one soldier at Culloden, Private John Tovey of

A later sketch of a British infantryman by Paul Sandby which captures his character magnificently.

British grenadiers as they perhaps should have looked.

Monro's 37th Foot, was all of fifty-nine when he had his jaw shot away, but he was exceptional, having been "born in the army" and presumably having no other home to go to. In theory there was no pension system unless a man was disabled in the service, but it is remarkable how many of those discharged after twenty years' good service were granted pensions on the rather loose grounds of being "worn out".

While the regulars were professional soldiers who fought the Jacobites simply because they were ordered to, they were assisted by a surprising number of loyalist volunteers. Prior to 1739 the army had of course policed the Highlands with a number of Independent Companies, familiarly known as the Black Watch, but in that year the companies were converted

A fine study of a French grenadier; most grenadiers in the French service were distinguished by bushy moustaches rather than caps. (Anne S.K. Brown Collection)

into the British Army's first Highland regiment. Despite a well-publicised mutiny in 1743 the experiment was adjudged a success, and in 1745 the Earl of Loudoun was given letters of service to recruit a second one, designated as the 64th Foot. The timing was unfortunate for the rising broke out while the regiment was still in the process of being raised and at least one company commanded by Cluny MacPherson, promptly defected to the rebels. On the other hand, the other companies, together with three depot companies of the Black Watch, provided a nucleus for the famous Argyle Militia. This was undoubtedly the most prominent of all the loyalist formations, but active opposition to the Jacks in Scotland was by no means confined to Clan Campbell and its allies. During most of the rebellion Inverness was held for the Crown by a whole army made up of independent companies recruited in the northern and western Highlands – and including the Skye MacDonalds. In combat these loyalist Highlanders generally proved to be as brittle as might be expected of any ill-trained and poorly motivated levies, but when stiffened by regulars and properly led, they could be quite effective – and never more so than at Culloden, where Captain Colin Campbell of Ballimore, with a company of his own 64th Highlanders, a Black Watch company under Dugald Campbell of Auchrossan and two militia companies, made a substantial contribution to the rebel defeat.

The same, obviously, was true of the various provincial regiments raised by patriotic noblemen and committees in England and the Scottish Lowlands. The most important of the latter were the Highland Independent Companies, and in the Lowlands the Earl of Home's brigade, made up of provincial regiments from Edinburgh, Glasgow and Paisley, which successfully defended the Forth crossings late in 1745 and afterwards fought at Falkirk. Even the various rag-tag local

'Charge your bayonet breast high', as demonstrated by a recreated member of Pulteney's 13th Foot. This was the preparatory position adopted immediately after firing one last close-range volley at the enemy.

volunteer militias such as the Derby Blues or the Aberdeen militia were of some use, in that they could be employed on rudimentary constabulary duties which would otherwise have had to be performed by regulars.

Some soldiers, however, were not volunteers. At the height of the emergency in 1745 two acts were rushed through parliament encouraging magistrates to conscript "all able-bodied me who do not follow or exercise any lawful calling or employment." In other words, parish constables were encouraged to turn over all their drunks, wastrels and petty criminals without the trouble of remanding them to the next assizes, and better yet, for each recruit delivered up they received a bounty of £3 paid into the vestry account, which was supposedly for the upkeep of any dependents left behind by the reluctant hero. Popular prejudice notwithstanding, the army was actually fairly particular about where it found its recruits, and, though backed up by a ferocious code of punishments, military discipline was consequently lightly administered. Both officers and soldiers therefore viewed these shabby conscripts with a distinctly jaundiced eye. All of

'Push your bayonet': though apparently unwieldy this method of bayonet fighting, based on earlier pike drills, was extremely effective when practised en masse.

them were discharged as soon as their services could decently be dispensed with, and in the meantime, those belonging to the Culloden regiments were allotted all the dirty jobs such as battlefield clearance and burial details, and prisoner handling – with unhappy results. It was the wretched "vestry men" for example who were assigned to act as guards on the transports carrying Jacobite prisoners to London.

As for the Jacobites, throughout its existence the army was organised into discrete Highland and Lowland divisions. The first was made up of the Gaelic-speaking clan regiments from the West Highlands, most of which had fought at Prestonpans, while the latter, perhaps a little surprisingly, not only comprised the regiments raised all the way along the east coast from Banff to Dundee, but also included units such as the Atholl Brigade which had a fair claim to being Highlanders but were widely considered to be steadier and a lot less "wild" than the western clans, such as the MacDonalds and Camerons. Nevertheless, well aware that it was the Highlanders who had so swiftly and convincingly not merely defeated but utterly destroyed General Cope's army at Prestonpans, the rebels

A recreated section of the Royals.

consciously took to referring to themselves as the *Highland Army* and dressing accordingly.

Whether, to quote Lieutenant General Henry Hawley, those actually standing in the ranks were indeed "true highlanders" or merely "lowlanders and other arrant scum", recruitment for the Jacobite Army was necessarily somewhat haphazard.

Some were indeed genuine volunteers. On 12 September 1745 the Laird of Grant's factor in Glen Urquhart complained that "last night two of Shewglie's sons went off to the Highland armie with a dozen young fellows, amongst whom were Alexander Grant in Inchbrin... and James Grant his brother, who were the only two worthwhile went with Shewglie's sons; for all the rest was only servants to some of the tenants." On the other hand, not many clansmen had the opportunity to freely decide whether to come out as the Glen Urquhart men did. At the other end of the scale was Donald Beaton from Tiree, a petty thief who was "with ye rebels 2 or 3 days and knows not the Regt."

As one of Robert Louis Stevenson's characters wryly declared, "when the piper plays the clan must dance" whether that meant old men, young boys or Donald Beaton. All were bound to follow their chieftain, willing or

Gunner, Royal Artillery, c. 1742.

Donald MacDonald, one of the Black Watch mutineers executed in 1743.

not and the Reverend William Gordon of Alvie declared that out of 43 of his parishioners caught up in the rising, only three had gone voluntarily while the rest were forced out by "burning their houses, carrying off their cattle and breaking their heads."

Even when the Jacobite leaders had no hold over their people, whether as chieftains or as landlords, a rudimentary form of conscription was sometimes attempted. In the North-East of Scotland, young Lord Lewis Gordon demanded that landowners should turn out one able-bodied man, properly clothed and equipped, for every £100 [Scots] on their rent roll. This obviously caused some difficulty and a degree of coercion had to be applied. Initially Gordon tried quartering his men in the refractory districts, quite literally eating all concerned out of house and home until they took the hint, but threats of burning their thatch soon produced quicker results, and in December 1745 Gordon wrote that: "Although I have got some volunties, I assure you that att least two thirds of the men I have raised is by the stipulation att first agreed on, and all those that have not as yet sent their quotas have been wrote to in very strong terms." Consequently, as an eyewitness noted, "the burning of a single house or farm stack in a Parish terrified the whole, so that they would quickly send in their proportion, and by this means, with the few that joined as volunteers, he [Gordon] raised near 300 men called the Strathboggy Battalion in the country thereabouts."

In some cases, many of those concerned escaped by simply stumping up £5 sterling in lieu of a man – which is what a number of observers unkindly suggested the Jacobites really wanted, but a substantial number of the actual recruits were paid a bounty to serve. In Banffshire alone, where a substantial part of the Strathbogie Regiment was raised, no fewer than one third of those recorded as serving in the rebellion were recorded as having been "hired out by the county". Similarly, in Forfarshire Charles Mather, a ploughman from Montrose was "hired by a farmer in his stead" to serve in Lord Ogilvy's Regiment although once again David Scott from Forfar was "hired by the county."

Well aware of this practice, the authorities were surprisingly careful to distinguish between ordinary rebels and those men who were hired out. Both the genuine volunteers and those who claimed to have been forced out were

A loyalist Highland officer, by McIan, after a contemporary print by Van Gucht.

Jacobite officer with Spanish musket, by Robert McIan.

unequivocally treated as rebels. The hired substitutes on the other hand appear to have very largely been recognised as such. Since they had joined the Jacobite Army for money rather than out of any commitment to the Pretender or any of his confederates, they were clearly no threat to the state and there was therefore no point in treating them as such. A quite disproportionate number of those taken prisoner were therefore simply released – or transferred into the ranks of the British Army.

The clothing and equipment of the rival armies was at once distinctive and yet once again fundamentally similar. Perceptions of the British army are unduly coloured by the well-known marionette-like figures of the 1742 Cloathing Book, which was actually laid out as a schematic record of individual regimental distinctions, rather than a realist depiction of the soldiers wearing those uniforms. Consequently, their uniforms are contrasted unfavourably with that of their rebel opponents and claimed to be tight and cumbersome, but eyewitness sketches and descriptions of soldiers on campaign show a very different picture. Like all British soldiers before and since they appear as shabby but comfortably dressed figures. The fancy lace was stripped off, the tricorne hats slouched at the first opportunity and not one of them appears to have looked exactly the same as the next.

They all did wear red coats of course and by way of distinction their opponents wore tartan ones – any tartan would do just so long as it was tartan. The clansmen obviously wore Highland clothes as a matter of course, but those conscripts and hired men levied out beyond the Highland line, were also ordered to be "well clothed with short cloathes, plaid, new shoes and three pair of hose and accoutered with shoulder ball gun, pistols and sword".

This accords exactly with the popular image of Jacobite soldiers, but while it was not too difficult to find enough tartans and plaids, all too-often the equipping of them foundered on the impossibility of finding large numbers of swords and pistols. Some probably did carry them, but the majority were principally armed with firelocks and bayonets, just as their regular opponents were – sometimes literally so.

As the army readied itself for the march into England hundreds of targes, the round leather-covered shields carried by swordsmen were ordered from Edinburgh workshops, and officers of Lowland regiments such as Lord Ogilvy's were ordered to take them up, but once again we have no way of knowing how many were actually delivered and the corresponding swords were also in short supply. The Laird of Grant's factor commented for example that "Lord Lovet is making ready to march. He has given orders to all his men to be in readiness, and has a good many smiths and tinkers preparing there arms and targes", but the quantity and quality of both may be doubted, for some very poor quality swords of the period are to be found in modern collections.

An admittedly hostile witness, Patrick Crichton of Woodhouselee, described how those clansmen who captured Edinburgh in mid-September were armed with a wide and varied selection of firearms, many of them fowling pieces and some "tyed with puck threed [string] to the stock, some withowt locks and some matchlocks." Others had only rusty swords or Lochaber axes and inevitably there were also the pitchforks and scythes which were an obligatory accessory of any rebel army north or south of the border. Effectively however it was only the officers and the gentlemen standing in the front ranks who were armed with the full combination of basket-hilted broadsword, targe and pistol popularly associated with clansmen. Most telling of all, Cumberland reported that his clearance squads had recovered a total of 2,320 firelocks from the battlefield of Culloden but only 192 broadswords. No doubt many of the firelocks were discarded by men who managed to make their escape from the field, but with Jacobite casualties estimated at upwards of 1,500 men this means that slightly less than one in eight of those rebels killed or captured there was carrying a broadsword.

For most Jacobite soldiers their principal weapon was a military calibre firelock and a bayonet to go with it, and this And this point is graphically underlined by the discovery in recent archaeological excavations of the remains of a French bayonet near the Well of the Dead, where so many of the clansmen died.

General Cope brought 1,467 men to Prestonpans and nearly all of their weapons passed into Jacobite hands. Obviously many were scavenged by those who fought there, but sufficient remained for both John Gordon of Glenbuchat's Regiment and the first battalion of Lord Ogilvy's Regiment to be wholly armed with .75 calibre land pattern firelocks and bayonets taken from Cope's army. Over time most units however received French ones. Some 1,500 to 1,600 stand of arms -firelock and bayonet complete – were landed at Montrose by blockade runners in October alone [probably of the model 1717], and other large shipments followed, including some Spanish weapons landed at Peterhead and on Barra. The result was that by the time Culloden was fought the whole army was fought the whole army was properly equipped with .69 calibre French or Spanish military firelocks and bayonets. Indeed, in the immediate aftermath of Culloden, Cumberland directed that freed prisoners from his own forces were to be temporarily issued with captured French and Spanish muskets and accoutrements.

Prior to 1746, the British Army's tactical philosophy simply came down to forming up in a line three ranks deep, moving into fairly close proximity to the enemy – 50 metres or less – and then halting and blazing away until fire superiority was achieved and the opposing side, whether French, Spanish or anyone else, conceded defeat. The conventional view, with a wealth of precedent to back it up, was that winning the firefight depended on being able to maintain a steady rolling fire, and the chosen method of delivering that fire was called Platooning, as described by Humphrey Bland in his influential *Treatise of Military Discipline* and formally laid down in the official 1728 *Regulations*. This battle drill required a battalion to be divided into a series of ad hoc platoons each of between twenty to thirty men who would then fire in a pre-arranged sequence rippling up and down the line. Given sufficient practice and the incentive provided by sheer terror, it was just about possible to loose off four or even five rounds a minute; but under stress soldiers will always fire high, and this rate of fire was not only wasteful but unsustainable, since it was common to go into action with as few as twelve rounds. Instead, officers and NCOs were trained to control the firing so that the men remained calm and levelled their firelocks properly instead of firing

A particularly ragged looking clansman, or even a Lowland volunteer, armed with a so-called Lochaber axe. Despite its designation this form of pole-weapon was usually made in Aberdeen, and considerable numbers were furnished by the burgh for the Jacobite Army in 1715.

rapidly into the air. In this regard individual platoons were obviously much more manageable than complete battalions. Despite its limitations, the tactic of platooning was therefore effective enough in conventional operations, especially against the French, whose fire discipline was notoriously bad, but employing it against Highlanders simply did not work, and worse still was probably downright dangerous. The deliberately paced rate of fire, while well adapted to maintaining a sustained firefight, simply could not kill enough clansmen quickly enough to stop a fast-moving Highland charge.

Consequently, a radical change of tactics was called for, and at Culloden heavy massed battalion volleys would be employed instead. There was of course an obvious danger that if the volley was badly timed and the Highlanders ignored their casualties to press home the charge, the whole battalion might still be reloading as the attack came in. The answer, pioneered by at least some units at Falkirk, was to direct the front rank not to reload after that first volley, but instead to charge their bayonets as soon as they had fired, thus protecting the second and third ranks as they reloaded and poured in a succession of volleys at point-blank range. In fact Monro's as we have seen even managed to get off two full volleys at Culloden before charging bayonets.

By contrast, instead of trying to win the firefight before closing with the enemy, the Jacobites attempted – with considerable success at Prestonpans – to rely instead on speed and sheer intimidation by attacking immediately, sword in hand, not necessarily in the expectation of literally carving through the opposing ranks, but instead inducing panic. Ideally, it might be accomplished as it was at Prestonpans by rolling up a flank, but what is striking about the Highland charge is how hit and miss it was and how costly it could be even if successful. At Killiecrankie in 1689 Sir Ewen Cameron of Lochiel's Regiment had rolled down a steep hillside to literally annihilate General Mackay's own regiment in what is regarded as the quintessential example of a Highland charge, but it cost the Camerons fully half of their number in killed and wounded.

Notwithstanding their own bombast, the Jacobites themselves were all-too keenly aware of the cost of simply flinging themselves at the enemy head on ad hoping for the best, and according to Lord George Murray, prompted by the near fiasco at Falkirk in January 1746:

"The best of the Highland officers, whilst they remained at Falkirk after the battle, were absolutely convinced that, except they could attack the enemy at a very considerable advantage, either by surprise or by some strong situation of ground, or a narrow pass, they could not expect any great success, especially if their numbers were no ways equal, and that a body of regular troops was absolutely necessary to support them, when they should at any time go in sword in hand; for they were sensible, that without more leisure and time to discipline their own me, it would not be possible to make them keep their ranks, or rally soon enough upon any sudden emergency, so that any small number of the enemy, either keeping in a body when they were in confusion or rallying would deprive them of a victory, even after they had done their best."

The body of regular troops they had in mind were of course the French, but there were never enough of them. By the time the Jacobites got to Culloden they had been joined by various contingents of French regulars run through the Royal Navy's blockade. In addition to a variety of technical specialists such as artillerymen and engineers, and military advisors such as Nicholas Glasgoe [despite his name an Irishman born in France] assigned to "discipline the militia" ie; to train rebel units such as Lord Ogilvy's Regiment, there were eventually two weak infantry battalions and a squadron of cavalry, all drawn from the Famous Irish Brigade.

This had its origins in the Jacobite War of the 1690s when the then King James exchanged Irish recruits for French regulars. Afterwards the exiles and their sons soldiered on in the French army but over the years the Brigade increasingly relied on French recruits and a very high proportion of the mercenaries serving in the ranks of these so-called Irish units were actually deserters and turned prisoners of war. In fact, according to the French ambassador to the rebels, over half of the Irish who fought at Culloden were turned prisoners, seemingly members of Guise's 6th Foot captured at Fort Augustus, hence the desperate fight they made. Fortunately, although condemned to death almost as a matter of course most of the survivors were released on the intercession of the Reverend Alexander MacBean, who testified to the poor treatment they had received while in rebel hands and the pressure placed upon them to enlist.

One of the two infantry battalions was a composite formation initially made up of picquets or company-sized detachments drawn from three different Irish regiments; *Dillon, Lally* and *Rooth*. These first three Irish Picquets fought at Falkirk and were subsequently joined by a picquet from the *Regiment de Berwick*, although a second *Berwick* picquet was captured after landing in the far north of Scotland. The other battalion was Lord John Drummond's newly raised regiment, the *Royal Eccossois*, which landed more or less intact at Montrose. Two companies of the regiment, including the grenadiers, served with the Irish Picquets at the battle of Falkirk, while the remainder were left guarding Stirling. Drummond, who was in overall command of the French contingent, had a commission to raise a second battalion for his regiment while in Scotland and certainly picked up some recruits although the extent of his success is uncertain. The regiment did, however, have a distinctive uniform. Instead of the usual knee-length coats, they had Scottish style hip-length jackets, and Scottish blue bonnets instead of tricorne hats. Their jackets were also blue, with red cuffs, in contrast to the red coats worn by the Irish regiments.

Both they and the Irish were of course conventionally equipped with firelock muskets and bayonets. French tactical doctrines fitted in very well with Jacobite ones. Essentially the French Army's favoured methods boiled down to manoeuvring in column, but then deploying and fighting in a four-rank deep battle line. Like the Highlanders they generally relied upon shock action with the bayonet rather than firepower. This was partly down to a not unreasonable perception that standing around exchanging fire was ineffective – the great *Marechal* de Saxe once acidly commented that he had seen complete battalion volleys which killed no more than four men – although it was also held as an article of faith that French soldiers were naturally impetuous and best suited to precipitous assaults. This preoccupation with offensive tactics led to a certain *laissez faire* attitude towards musketry. If it did come down to a firefight the usual practice was to commence firing by ranks and then after the initial series of volleys to continue with a *feu a la billebaude* which essentially meant every soldier loading and firing in his own time.

In addition to the infantry, it was also intended to ship over the whole of the cavalry regiment *Fitzjames Cavallerie* or Fitzjames's Horse, but most of their transports were captured by the Royal Navy and only the equivalent of a single squadron was actually landed at Aberdeen. They were heavy cavalry with cuirasses or iron breastplates worn under their coats and finding suitable horses for them proved to be a problem even after Lord Kilmarnocks "Horse Grenadiers" were dismounted ordered to turn theirs over, before reconstituting themselves as a regiment of Footguards Consequently, only about half of Fitzjames's troopers were mounted at Culloden and the remainder presumably fought on foot with the Picquets.

This was unfortunate, for the rebels had always been short of cavalry – in conventional terms at least – but in practical terms this actually made little difference, for although an English volunteer named John Daniel acknowledged his dismay at Falkirk when "we were about four hundred light Horse ordered to face the enemy's dragoons" the prospect of their doing so was quite exceptional.

Regular cavalry regiments comprised six troops – the mounted equivalent of companies – which in battle were paired off into three squadrons, which normally formed up in six men [and horses] deep. In 1746 they were classed as either horse or dragoons. The former were the more prestigious and reckoned to be true battle or heavy cavalry, but experience as long ago as 1689 had shown their big horses were insufficiently robust for Scottish conditions. Dragoons on the other hand were originally mounted infantry and traditionally mounted on cheaper but sturdier nags. In theory they were primarily intended to be employed for scouting or outpost duties. Over the years however in what was to be a depressingly familiar cycle, this particular role was to be largely abandoned in favour of charging into battle, locked up knee to knee as battle cavalrymen. Consequently, though the

British Army enjoyed an overwhelming numerical superiority in the mounted arm throughout the campaign, its commanders consistently failed to make proper use of that superiority in the all-important scouting and intelligence-gathering role – an omission which is all the more remarkable in that Generals Cope, Wade and Hawley all had a cavalry background. Only some of the provincial and volunteer militia units, most notably perhaps Kingston's 10th Horse [whose title ironically enough classed them as heavies], were employed as proper light cavalry and they, for all their later reputation, were usually outclassed as scouts by their rebel counterparts.

In fact, apart from carrying out escort duties, the rebel cavalry were primarily employed on scouting and picquet duty and after a shaky start got to be very good at it. This is perhaps all the more remarkable given that Jacobite units were invariably small, and with the exception of the Lifeguards never amounted to more than a couple of troops apiece. Consequently both horses and riders were invariably overworked – one English eyewitness scathingly declared "they have such scurvy Horses that I have seen several of them exert all their Vigour to bring them to a Gallop, In spite of which the poor Beasts immediately fell into a Pace more suited to their Age and Infirmities." That particular problem was less to do with the origins of the horses than the simple fact that horses are surprisingly delicate animals and need proper looking after. In any winter campaign, hard usage and bad weather saw heavy losses in horses and left those who survived in poor condition. It certainly did not help, however, that some of the best horses available to the rebels – those captured from Cope's dragoons at Prestonpans, were most of them assigned to haul the army's cannon!

The Jacobite artillery is all-too frequently dismissed as useless, yet as General Hawley declared when setting out for Stirling, to march without artillery "would be silly". If anything the rebels were embarrassed by the number of cannon they dragged around but once again it needs to be emphasised that its performance at Culloden was not hampered by a multiplicity of calibres complicating the ammunition supply, as suggested by John Prebble. There were indeed a confusing variety of cannon found after the battle, but many were parked at Culloden House and all but one of those actually emplaced on the moor were 3-pounders. Ironically enough, most of them were in fact British guns originally captured by the French at the battle of Fontenoy in 1745 and then shipped across to arm the rebels. They were therefore identical to those being used on the other side of the moor by Cumberland's gunners.

The Royal Artillery, as always, prided itself on being the most professional of the services – as indeed it had to be – and by way of demonstrating that it took its orders from the Board of Ordnance, its officers and men wore blue coats instead of red. Its organisation was necessarily looser or rather more flexible than that of the infantry, although the basic administrative unit, as in the infantry, was still the company. There was no fixed allocation of guns to a company and gunners were expected to be able to serve whatever cannon were deemed appropriate, or at least available for the job in hand. At Culloden, therefore, Captain Lieutenant John Godwin's company was equipped with those light 3-pounders, selected for their mobility on Scotland's notoriously bad roads. When the company was afterwards redeployed to Flanders however they left this particular train of guns in Scotland to be taken over by their successors, while they themselves re-equipped with heavier pieces more suitable to continental warfare.

Ammunition for these guns generally took three forms. The first and commonest was roundshot or cannonballs; solid iron spheres 3 inches in diameter. This was used by both sides at the outset of the battle but its effectiveness was compromised both by the extreme range at which the guns were firing and by the uneven nature of the ground which made observation difficult, and also because its softness inhibited the usual ability of the rounds to skip along just above ground level, just as a stone skims across still water. Once the rebels came closer in the Royal Artillery were able to switch to grape and cannister. The latter was literally a tin canister, rather like an oversized shotgun cartridge, which burst apart on leaving the muzzle spraying the oncoming target with musket balls. [The finds from the 2005 excavation included the lid from one such cannister]. Also used at Culloden was grape or grapeshot. Made famous by Napoleon's boast of a "whiff of grapeshot", this was normally the Navy's equivalent of cannister, employing fewer but larger rounds of cast iron rather than lead – intended to pierce wooden bulwarks and barricades. Why it was used at Culloden is not known, but it may have been begged from the Navy to cover a shortage of ordinary cannister.

One form of ammunition unique to the British army at Culloden was a bombshell – an explosive round lobbed from a stubby little mortar. Normally it was used in assaulting fortified positions since it could drop a shell over a wall or into a trench, but at Culloden, Godwin's men used them to fire over the heads of their own front line and drop them into the middle of the massed clansmen beyond, thereby giving rise to stories of hidden batteries.

In summary, the two armies probably had more in common than might at first appear. Both were similar in their basic organisation and equipment, and arguably, geography aside were similar in the social origins of both their officers and their rank and file. The rebels, obviously, were at first very poorly equipped and barely trained but overcame this at Prestonpans by simply hurling themselves at their opponents and gaining the day by speed and panic. Much as they boasted of their victory and similarly played up the shambolic affair at Falkirk four months later, the more intelligent of the Jacobite leaders recognised that in both battles they had been lucky, that such tactics could not be relied upon and were likely to be hideously costly if unaided by fog or a wild thunderstorm. It is one of the tragedies of Culloden that they anticipated its result months before.

CHAPTER VIII

The Battlefields of the '45 Today

I Prince Charles and the '45

Culloden lies just 5 miles outside the centre of Inverness, and so the Highland capital forms an obvious base for visiting both the battlefield and its environs. Though it is accessible by air and rail, Inverness is best approached by road since this not only allows the visitor a considerable degree of flexibility on the spot, but also affords the opportunity to visit most of the related sites en route.

In fact, by starting the tour at Edinburgh it can very appropriately open with a visit to the battlefield of Prestonpans (21 September 1745), a few miles to the east of

Monument to the Battle of Prestonpans, located close by the position occupied by General Cope's right wing.

the city, before heading north to Falkirk (17 January 1746) and then straight up the A9 to Inverness, with optional stops to view the earlier battlefields of Sheriffmuir (1715) and Killiecrankie (1689), and an essential stop to visit Ruthven Barracks, near Kingussie.

Prestonpans lies on the north side of the A1 trunk road, east of Edinburgh. The site is easily identified from the A1 by a large artificial mound formed when part of the battlefield was levelled to create the playing fields attached to the Meadowmill Sports Centre.

The village of Prestonpans is well signposted from the A1 and best approached along the A198. A stone cairn by the roadside, inscribed with the date 1745, marks the approximate position of General Cope's extreme right flank. Immediately beside the cairn is a sign which quite erroneously points south to the 'battlesite'. Of itself the sign is totally misleading since the fighting took place to the north, but it does take the visitor to the spacious sports centre car park and the aforementioned mound. Since the battlefield is even flatter than Culloden, the top of the mound provides a good vantage point to get the overall feel of the place and to identify the few salient features. At first glance the battlefield is rather unprepossessing and might appear to have been totally destroyed by modern development, but in reality this is a pretty faithful reflection of its eighteenth-century character as a semi-industrial landscape in which cornfields were interspersed with salt pans and coal pits and everything that went with them.

Significantly one of the surviving features from 1745 is the trackbed of the Seton Wagon-way, along which General Cope formed his army. This crosses the A198 a little to the east of the 1745 cairn. Now a cycle path, it provides a convenient walking route to the church at Tranent on the hillside to the south of the A1. The

Colonel Gardiner's house at Prestonpans. The unfortunate Colonel commanded the 13th Dragoons and died in his own garden.

Gardiner's monument, erected in Victorian times despite a romantic revival of Jacobite sentiment.

Monument to the Battle of Falkirk, situated close to General Hawley's right wing.

churchyard, now somewhat enlarged for obvious reasons, was occupied as a Jacobite outpost on the day before the battle. From the church, walk westwards to reach Birsley Brae, otherwise known as 'Johnnie Cope's Road' since the unfortunate General retreated along it after the battle. Descending the hill by way of the road and then crossing the footbridge over the A1 will bring visitors to the handsomely restored Bankton House, with its distinctive ochre yellow walls. The house is private property, but is skirted by a footpath running alongside the railway line which passes a monument to Colonel Gardiner, whose home it was, before returning to the Meadowmill.

Falkirk is a relatively unspoilt battlefield and best approached from the A803, which passes through the town itself. Towards the western end of the town turn south on to the B816 where it branches off beside lock 16 on the Forth and Clyde Canal. After about a kilometre the B816 turns sharply right (west), but ignoring this turn carry straight on under a prominent railway bridge and canal viaduct to ascend a very steep wooded hillside. The narrow road leads eventually to the battle's monument just above Greenbank Farm. The monument is very helpfully situated at the top of the ravine which protected General Hawley's right flank, and a long narrow strip of woodland extending to the south must lie pretty well on top of the position briefly occupied by his front line before it was tumbled eastwards down the hill.

Both Prestonpans and Falkirk are covered in greater detail in the author's *Battles of the Scottish Lowlands*, as is Sheriffmuir, a short distance off the A9 above Dunblane. Other than the advent of the ubiquitous forestry plantations, Sheriffmuir is largely as it was in 1715, but the same cannot be said of Killiecrankie, further to the north. Unfortunately, the A9 not only slashes straight across the battlefield, but substantially overlies the ground occupied by the unfortunate General Mackay in 1689. (The visitor centre maintained by the National Trust is not located on the battlefield, but in the Pass of Killiecrankie itself.) Viscount Dundee's Jacobite Army was initially drawn up on a natural ledge above and to the east of the road, and the steepness of the slope which it charged down can easily be appreciated while driving by – stopping or driving slowly is not recommended. Killiecrankie was in fact the only battle in which the popular image of clansmen rushing down a hillside upon their red-coated foes like an avalanche of steel was actually realized.

II The Battle That Never Was

The Pass of Killiecrankie effectively formed the southern limit of Jacobite territory in the weeks leading up to Culloden, and just beyond it is Blair Castle, unsuccessfully besieged by Lord George Murray. The A9 at this point bypasses the village, but visitors should follow signposts to Blair Atholl. The castle is still in the ownership of the Atholl family and is open to the public.

Further north by Kingussie, and clearly visible just to the east of the A9, are the impressive ruins of Ruthven Barracks. In the care of Historic Scotland, the site is currently unmanned and accessible at any time. Probably best known for the fact that the rebel army disbanded there after Culloden, it also deserves to be

Ruthven Barracks as it is today, well sited on the motte of a former medieval castle.

remembered for the gallant stand made by Sergeant Molloy and his twelve men on 30 August 1745:

> Yesterday there appeared in the little Town of Ruthven above 300 Men of the Enemy, and sent Proposals to me to surrender this Redoubt, upon Condition that I should have Liberty to carry off Bag and Baggage. My answer was, that I was too old a Soldier to surrender a Garrison of such strength without bloody Noses. They threatened hanging me and my Men for Refusal. I told them I would take my Chance. This Morning they attacked me about twelve'o'Clock, by my Information with about 150 Men: They attacked the Fore-Gate and Sally-Port, and attempted to set the Sally-Port on Fire, with some old Barrels and other Combustibles, which took Blaze immediately; but the Attempter lost his life by it. They drew off about half an Hour after Three … I lost one Man shot through the Head by foolishly holding his Head too high over the Parapet, contrary to orders. I prevented the Sally-Port taking Fire by pouring Water over the Parapet. I expect another Visit this Night, I am informed … but I shall give them the warmest Reception my weak Party can afford. I shall hold out as long as possible.

In fact Molloy held out until 11 February 1746, which was a great deal better than his counterpart at Inverness Castle, Major George Grant, who lasted just a couple of days. Medieval in origin, Inverness Castle was reconstructed by General Wade as a fortified barracks, to form the northern end of the 'Chain' of fire bases along the

The rear gate at Ruthven which the Jacobites tried to burn down, until Sergeant Molloy's men shot them down from the loophole in the flanking tower.

Great Glen. It was, however, blown up by the rebels after its capture. The present 'castle', though occupying the original site and still conveying some impression of its dominant position, is in fact a nineteenth-century municipal building.

The other 'Chain' forts have fared equally badly. Fort Augustus, having been badly damaged during the rebellion, eventually became a Cistercian abbey and school, but at the present time is in private hands. Some of the original remains but access is uncertain. Fort William for its part was substantially demolished to make way for a railway station, although some walls and bastions remain, and the governor's office has been preserved and reconstructed in the nearby West Highland Folk Museum.

Turning to the east, the ruins of Strathbogie or Huntly Castle, lying just outside the town of Huntly on the A92 Aberdeen to Inverness road, are certainly worth a visit, if only to appreciate the magnificent carving above the doorway. Now roofless, the castle was occupied by 2/Royals and serves to represent the British Army's jumping-off point for the final approach march. Fochabers and the Spey crossings have changed out of all recognition since 1746. The neat village which at present greets travellers is in fact a splendid example of a late eighteenth-century 'new town'.

III Night March

Although the intrepid may care to attempt to retrace the Jacobite Army's stumbling footsteps across country on a dark night, there is little or no tangible evidence of its passing, and Cumberland's main encampment at Balblair, perhaps not inappropriately, is now a caravan park. Ironically, the only real location of interest is the British cavalry's cantonments out at Auldearn. Once again there are no reminders of their stay, but the village was also the scene of an important and hard-fought battle in 1645 when the Royalist Marquess of Montrose was attacked and very nearly beaten by the Scottish government's forces led by Sir John Hurry. Not directly relevant to the story of the '45, it is an interesting battle-site and well worth the minor diversion to view it.

While the village has substantially changed over the last 300 years and nothing of the original now remains except the ruins of the old church, the battlefield itself is pretty well untouched. A good vantage point, maintained by the National Trust for Scotland, is the Castle Hill, topped by the Boath Doo'cot (dovecot). There is a small car park for visitors at the bottom of the hill and the unmanned site is accessible at all times. Be aware, however, that the map on the frequently vandalized information board is not particularly accurate. The Castle Hill was occupied by Royalist troops, but most of the fighting took place on the low but surprisingly dominant Garlic Hill immediately to the west, and in the ditches and back gardens of the village which then lay on a north–south alignment, rather than from east to west along the former route of the A92, which now avoids rather than crosses the battlefield. A good account can be found in the author's *Auldearn, 1645*. Essentially, however, taking the Royalists by surprise, Sir John Hurry's forces seized Garlic Hill at dawn or shortly afterwards, and then tried to crack open a defensive line set up in the village. In the meantime the surprised Royalists assembled their main body to the east of the village, and then passing around it launched successful counter-attacks on both flanks of Hurry's main position on Garlic Hill.

IV High Noon on a Blasted Heath

Culloden Moor itself is best approached along the B9006 road. Although originating in Inverness itself, this road can be directly accessed either from the A9 if approaching from the south, or from the A92 Aberdeen–Inverness road if coming from the east. Both routes are well signposted although there is no consistency in the distances displayed on the various signs. While most visitors to the site will obviously arrive by car or coach, a bracing walk up the 5 miles of road from Inverness is entirely feasible and heartily recommended if time allows – the return journey is downhill. One of the attractions of walking rather than driving this route is that exactly the same road was used by Jacobite troops marching to the battlefield – and escaping from it afterwards.

Something between a third and a half of the Culloden battlefield is currently in the care of the National Trust for Scotland, with the remainder still in private hands. Since the first edition was published in 2005 the National Trust for Scotland has carried out a radical overhaul of facilities at the site and the way in which the battlefield is presented and interpreted.

A forestry plantation was cleared of trees some years ago and considerable efforts are being made to eradicate the secondary growth of shrubs and heather which until recently obscured much of the battlefield and its true character. Similarly, although

Another view of the moor which probably provides a fair idea of its original appearance as an area of rough grazing rather than heather moorland. The Jacobite Army began the battle where the line of trees can now be seen on the sky-line.

the old Inverness road that slashed across the moor in 1746 has been diverted to carry modern traffic clear of the burial area (although it is still by no means clear of the battlefield), its course can still be traced quite easily and the Trust plans to restore it to its original condition at the time of the battle.

The starting point for any visit will inevitably be the new visitor centre which unlike the old has been situated clear of the main area of fighting and which offers world-class interpretative facilities as well as a splendid bookshop.

If visiting the moor as part of an organized group it is useful to first assemble the whole party in the car park and form into a single line. It is not necessary to deliberately space individuals, although they should not be touching. A coach-load of just over 30 visitors will represent the approximate frontage required by 100 British soldiers drawn up in 3 ranks, and will require to be multiplied by 3 or 4 times depending on the individual unit to get an idea of the front occupied. For Barrell's 4th Foot for example, with 325 rank and file, imagine that your group is in the centre of the battalion with another group of equal size to the right and left. Monro's on the other hand would require four such groups, real or imaginary, to

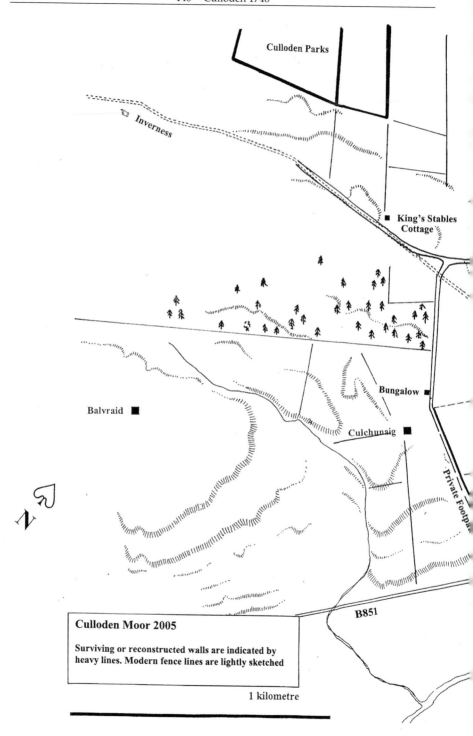

Culloden Parks

Inverness

King's Stables
Cottage

Bungalow

Balvraid

Culchunaig

Private Footpath

B851

N

Culloden Moor 2005

Surviving or reconstructed walls are indicated by
heavy lines. Modern fence lines are lightly sketched

1 kilometre

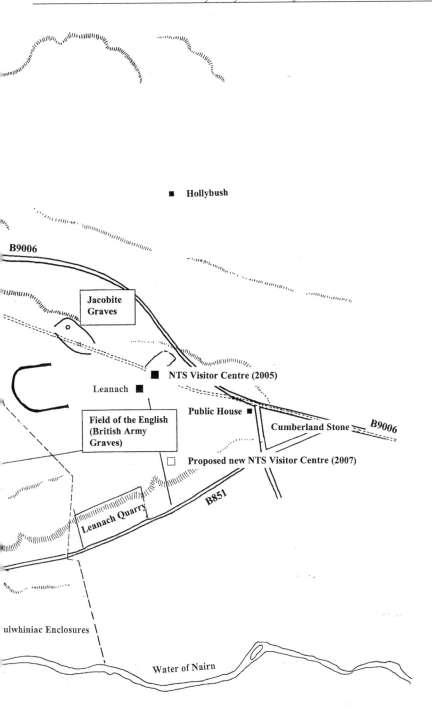

Hollybush

B9006

Jacobite Graves

NTS Visitor Centre (2005)

Leanach

Field of the English (British Army Graves)

Public House

Cumberland Stone

B9006

Proposed new NTS Visitor Centre (2007)

B851

Leanach Quarry

ulwhiniac Enclosures

Water of Nairn

represent it. A similar exercise may be carried out for the Jacobites, but remember that they tended to be drawn up in four ranks rather than three. Smaller groups will no doubt employ their ingenuity, and perhaps the goodwill of strangers, to make up for a lack of numbers.

In addition to a new network of footpaths corresponding much more closely to the original battle lines there are a number of original or reconstructed features of interest on the battlefield.

The most famous is the Old Leanach farmhouse. Once thought to have been standing at the time of the battle, recent research has revealed that the original turf-walled cottage was rebuilt in stone in about 1881, as accommodation for a resident guide, and archaeological evidence shows that what was once thought to be the adjacent remains of the 'red barn', traditionally burned by the Redcoats while full of rebel wounded, is a nineteenth-century kitchen-garden wall. It is also worth pointing out that not only did the original steading and its barn lie behind Cumberland's front line, just where the most savage fighting took place, but it is clear from contemporary correspondence that the site was used for some days afterwards as a *British* field hospital, not a rebel one.

Ahead of the 250th anniversary of the battle in 1996 the Trust reconstructed both the turf-walled Leanach enclosure and the lost northern corner of the dry-stone walled Culwhiniac enclosure. The southern wall of the Culwhiniac enclosures

View of the battlefield from the British front line. The Jacobites were initially drawn up along what is now the tree-line in the far distance. The uneven nature of the ground is readily apparent.

The reconstructed northern corner of the Culwhiniac enclosure wall, with the present Culchunaig in the background.

The remains of the southern wall of the Culwhiniac enclosure as it is today.

Looking along the British front line from Barrell's position on the left.

These farm buildings at Culchunaig date from the late nineteenth or early twentieth century and may occupy the original site, though Sandby's maps and sketches suggest the original may have been further south.

Looking forward from Barrell's position across the depression formed by what is now known as the Well of the Dead.

The Jacobite right wing position – on the tree-line – as viewed from the burial area.

actually survives, albeit in a ruined state and is supplemented by a modern post and wire fence. Comparison of Thomas Sandby's contemporary map confirms however that it still follows its original alignment, including its various kinks, all the way down the slope from Culchunaig to the Water of Nairn.

The wall terminates at Culchunaig at about spot height 163 on the 1:2500 Ordnance Survey map, just a few metres east of a very modern cottage, and it is in this area, currently outside the Trust's stewardship, where the Atholl Brigade took up its position on the extreme right of the Jacobite front line at the start of the battle. Fixing the corresponding position of the Jacobite left wing is less easy since a considerable number of new field boundaries have been created by the Culloden estates over the years as the moor was gradually brought into cultivation. Once again however the vital clue is provided by Thomas Sandby, whose map shows that the outer wall extended in a very straight line all the way down the hill to the front of Culloden House. That particular alignment now ends on the B9006 at King's Stables cottage, but in 1746 its eastern termination appears to have been further away from the road and is represented by the next field boundary back. Although the King's Stables, so-called because some dragoons were said to have been picketed in a nearby hollow after the battle, is in the ownership of the Trust, the remainder of the ground on the west side of the road, where the MacDonalds were posted, is still in private hands.

The reconstructed turf walls of the Leanach enclosure as viewed from the northern corner of the Culwhiniac enclosures.

The reconstructed corner of the Culwhiniac enclosure at the point where Ballimore's Highland Battalion ambushed the Royal Ecossois.

V Claymore!

As will have been apparent from the foregoing chapters, the battle of Culloden effectively consisted of two quite separate engagements and although much of both actions took place simultaneously, visitors will find it difficult to be in two places at once.

Depending on the time available there are two routes which can be followed. If time is relatively short or visitors are not as young as they once were, the easy option is to head out from the visitor centre, following the existing network of footpaths out as far as the Jacobite front line position, taking a nod to the scene of Hawley's action beyond Culchunaig and then returning along the B9006 to the centre. This is essentially the tour which will be described in this section, with the more intrepid alternative in the next.

The original British front line, pinpointed by Tony Pollard's archaeological investigations, actually stood a little way short of the cluster of mass graves placed on either side of what was the old road, just south of Leanach and Barrell's Regiment, and was actually drawn up just above what is now known as the Well of the Dead, before being overrun. Hemmed in by Huske's counter-attack and shot down in a deadly cross-fire this depression must have been choked with dead and wounded after the battle, hence its chilling sobriquet.

The burial area – presumably once the nearest parcel of ground dry enough to dig graves, is dominated by a large cairn dating from about 1881 and at the same

Probably the most accurate of the various rustic stones placed above the grave mounds in the 1880s.

time a number of individual headstones were placed on certain of the grave mounds, commemorating the various clans whose dead are assumed to lie there. Whilst serving as a very proper memorial it should not be assumed that the designations of graves to particular clans are accurate and as will become immediately apparent on looking about there are a considerable number of other graves, chiefly on the north side of the old road, which have no headstones.

From this area head towards the remaining Forestry Commission plantation west of Culchunaig, passing the reconstructed Leanach and Culwhiniac walls on the right. Neither are currently within the area of the battlefield managed by the Trust and closer inspection should only be undertaken with discretion and respect for the fact that the land is private property. The far boundary of the Trust site is the farm road linking Culchunaig with the B9006. This marks the approximate position of Jacobite front line when the battle began, although it was not quite on this alignment. Having reached this road you may either turn right towards Culchunaig, which will be described in the next section, or left towards the B9006. Lady Mackintosh's Regiment was drawn up across the B9006 somewhere between the junction and the King's Stables. Now return along the B9006 to the visitor centre, passing en route through the centre of Cumberland's front line. Approaching from this direction Campbell's Royal Scots Fusiliers will have stood on what is now the right side of the road and Price's 14th Foot on the left. The MacDonalds probably came to grief in what is now a lightly wooded area further out to the west.

Proceeding further down the road towards the visitor centre, the left flank of Sempill's 25th (Edinburgh) Regiment – now the King's Own Scottish Borderers – standing in the second line would have 'rested' on the road just short of the car-park entrance, with the far right of the second line standing on the site of the present Hollybush Farm. Ligonier's Regiment was originally drawn up in what is now the northern part of the car park itself.

The tour of the battlefield can either end there, or move on to the more ambitious phase.

The burial area and 1881 cairn, now cleared of both trees and secondary growth.

VI Blood on the Heather

To cover the scene of Hawley's action, proceed eastwards along the B9006 to a crossroads, marked by a pub, where refreshment may be sought before carrying on, and also by the Cumberland Stone – a large flat rock where the victorious general is variously said to have viewed the battle or sought some refreshment of his own. The former seems unlikely since he is known to have posted himself on the right of his front line, but it is possible he may have dined here afterwards. Refreshed or otherwise, turn right down the hill a short distance to join the B851 at the next crossroads. Turn right again and follow the road southwards past the Leanach Quarry. Although the exact route cannot be plotted with any real certainty, this is more or less the track followed by Hawley and his dragoons on 16 April 1746. The first of the walls to be breached by Campbell of Ballimore's Highlanders was just past the quarry. The footings of the second are, however, still extant not too far beyond. Leave the B851 at this point and begin climbing up to the moor along the footpath on the south (left) side of the wall. This footpath leads directly to Culchunaig. Depending on ground and weather conditions – and whatever is in the fields to the left, which are in private ownership – you may proceed directly to Culchunaig or strike out westwards across the fields to find the very prominent re-entrant across which Hawley's cavalrymen and the Jacobites faced each other. It will readily be appreciated that the strength of the rebel position was derived not so much from the physical obstacle posed by the 'ditch', but from the difficulty Hawley faced in establishing exactly what he was up against.

Even the oldest of the present buildings at Culchunaig obviously date from the late nineteenth or early twentieth centuries and as discussed in the main text it seems just possible, judging by Sandby's various maps and sketches, that the original steading may have been a little further to the south west. At any rate although some modern accounts of the battle identify the 'ditch' with what was described in 1867 as a 'hollow of some little depth bending around the Culchunaig farm steading on the east and north', it is clear that it would have been quite impossible to cram ten troops of dragoons into the 100 metre gap between the steading and the Culwhiniac wall. Instead, this particular hollow must be the one in which various Jacobite units, including Lord Lewis Gordon's men and the Prince's escort troop, sheltered during the bombardment.

A whole day should be allowed for a comprehensive visit to the battlefield, especially if it is intended to walk out from Inverness. In any event, as most of the moor is still as boggy as it was in 1746; a stout pair of boots is essential if it is intended to stray off the official paths. Otherwise the site *can* be comfortably viewed in a couple of hours, leaving ample time for a subsidiary visit to the quite magnificent Fort George (built in 1757) at nearby Ardersier.

Further Reading

There is of course no shortage of books on the '45, and John Prebble's classic *Culloden*, first published in 1961 and never out of print, cannot be bettered for its accessibility as a narrative and above all its human dimension to the battle.

After Culloden it was emigration rather than the infamous – and quite unconnected – clearances which depopulated the Highlands.

Nevertheless, the actual reconstruction of the battle is a little superficial and based on an outdated and now discredited model and like most fails to offer anything approaching a forensic examination of its military history. The present author's *Like Hungry Wolves* [London 1994] is the first modern study of the battle to combine extensive eyewitness testimony from both sides with a thorough study of contemporary tactics and above all the ground itself. This volume is of course heavily based on it, but since 1994 much important archaeological work has been carried out and any essential reading list must include Dr. Tony Pollard's *Culloden: The History and Archaeology of the Last Clan Battle* [Barnsley 2009].

As to the armies; one of the best dedicated studies of the Jacobite one remains the introductory volume of *Prisoners of the 45*, edited by Sir Bruce Gordon Seton and Jean Arnot [3 Volumes, Scottish History Society, Edinburgh 1928-1929], although the author's *The Scottish Jacobite Army 1745-46* [Oxford 2006] is modestly recommended, together with its companion *Cumberland's Culloden Army 1745-46* [Oxford 2012]. The latter provides a wide-ranging survey of the British Army throughout the campaign and is not to be confused with *Cumberland's Army: The British Army at Culloden* [Leigh on Sea 2006] , which focusses only on those regiments serving there and includes all known eyewitness accounts arranged regiment by regiment.

Index